For too long, we have ignored the signs of mass casualty attacks and refused to work together to "connect the dots." Rick has given us a road map to do just that. Every community in the nation would benefit from the lessons that Rick is teaching. We need to work together to prevent attacks, not just respond to them—and this book shows us how.

Captain Kevin Griger
Sarpy County Sheriff's Office

Human history is a chronicle of violence and the efforts to manage it. We are fully aware of many violent acts such as the Columbine massacre, 9/11, and numerous workplace incidents. The primary approaches to violence have been focused on installing security systems and implementing response strategies. However, the most effective way to face any disaster, even the current COVID-19 pandemic, is prevention. This playbook for violence prevention by Rick Shaw is exactly what we need to effectively manage human-made disasters. The book makes significant contributions with clearly designed network-based prevention systems that are supported by advanced technologies and "how-to" steps for prevention based on the numerous real-world experiences of experts. It is a must-read for school administrators, teachers, parents, business executives, government leaders, and all of us.

Dr. Sang M. Lee
Professor emeritus, University of Nebraska–Lincoln

"Tips," as we call it, is a way of life for me. It's what I do day in and day out. In an urban school district of 45,000 students, we receive thousands of reports annually. Dots get plotted every day with every report. Sometimes the dots get connected right away, and sometimes it takes a while, but eventually, they always do. For some of these kids, Tips is their lifeline. It's like there was one person who cared enough to submit a report—and that one report changed their world.

Tracy Alvarez
Coordinator of attendance advocacy & bullying prevention, Oklahoma City Public Schools

The First Preventers Playbook is an outstanding work that will help stop "bullying behaviors." I've worked with Rick Shaw and utilized Awareity's resources for many years now through our organization and have passed them on to more than 1,500 schools all across our nation. The research, thought, and work done by Rick and his team has helped save and change the lives of thousands of our kids. I've seen the direct results, so I know that I can honestly say this book will be a very valuable resource to any organization, school, administrator, teacher, or parent. Thank you, Rick, for helping our kids!

Kirk Smalley
President and cofounder, Stand for the Silent

The First Preventers Playbook *is essential reading for everyone. In the current landscape of violence, it is easy to feel disempowered and helpless, yet every person is capable of being a first preventer. In this important work, Rick Shaw demonstrates how we can prevent violence both as individuals and as a community.*

Dr. Nathan Brooks
Forensic psychologist and senior lecturer,
CQUniversity, Australia

Mr. Shaw's book provides easy reading and excellent guidance on the prevention of violent incidents at schools or in the workplace. Brief coverage of past events and the lessons learned leads into the need for and use of a threat assessment process. Its contents are beneficial for both those with and those without a background on the topic.

Branch Walton
Office of Naval Intelligence, Ret.; Secret Service, Ret.;
professor; corporate security director

This playbook is definitely needed in today's world to prevent potential tragedies from happening. The playbook allows all stakeholders to be on the same page when dealing with potentially bad incidents, and having a playbook on prevention can bring positive results for all involved. Community members will accept their roles better if we can be all on the same team. Having The First Preventers Playbook *will achieve this!*

Stephen P. Luce
Executive director, Indiana Sheriffs' Association, Ret.

Without question, this book will shape the future of violence prevention and positively change how we build our prevention architecture. For the first time, we now have the ability to develop actionable intelligence based on empirical data related to our day-to-day education and business operations. The First Preventers Playbook *aptly provides decision makers with new insights and tools in their effort to better prevent elevated acts of violence. This community-wide approach to preventing acts of violence is long overdue and will allow us to make the data-driven decisions needed to provide the safety our students and workforces deserve.*

Jason Thomas Destein
MS Criminal Justice, violence prevention strategist, adjunct professor

The First Preventers Playbook *by Rick Shaw is a great tool for schools implementing threat assessment management and prevention plans to reduce school violence. As a retired public school administrator who worked closely with Rick to implement the tools described in his book, I can attest to the importance of "connecting the dots" to maintain a safe learning environment. Once we began to connect the dots more efficiently, we became both better at prevention and mitigation efforts and better at designing student safety plans in efforts to reduce suspension and dropout rates. As I travel across Oklahoma to consult and train staff in school violence and threat assessment,* The First Preventer's Playbook *is absolutely in my tool bag.*

Tenna Whitsel
Retired School Administrator

Rick and I have had some interesting conversations over the years about prevention failures and improving intervention, disruption, and prevention efforts. His book is an excellent resource for anyone who is interested in how they can help their society prevent various acts of violence. Up until now, organizations in nearly every sector have not had the right tools, guidelines, and training so that anyone who is demonstrating warning signs (suicidal or homicidal) can be identified and helped before they escalate and attempt to do violence. Rick's book delivers a research-based overview of the six distinct but overlapping stages of preventing acts of violence and other incidents before they happen.

By educating, empowering, and equipping first preventers to collect, assess, connect the dots, and take the right actions to disrupt at-risk individuals on the pathway to violence, more violent incidents and tragedies can be prevented, and fewer first responders will have to put their lives on the line.

A First Preventers Program is certainly needed, and Rick's book certainly gives a comprehensive tool to do this. We need first preventers to assist and support first responders.

Totti Karpela
Director CTM, CETAP; founding member,
European Threat Assessment Professionals Association

RICK SHAW

THE
FIRST
PREVENTERS
PLAYBOOK

HOW TO
INTERVENE, DISRUPT, AND PREVENT
TRAGEDY BEFORE IT STRIKES

Advantage®

Published by Advantage, Charleston, South Carolina.
Member of Advantage Media Group.

ADVANTAGE is a registered trademark, and the Advantage colophon is a trademark of Advantage Media Group, Inc.

Printed in the United States of America.

10 9 8 7 6 5 4 3 2 1

ISBN: 978-1-64225-125-8
LCCN: 2020912718

Cover design by Megan Elger.
Layout design by Wesley Strickland.

This publication is designed to provide accurate and authoritative information in regard to the subject matter covered. It is sold with the understanding that the publisher is not engaged in rendering legal, accounting, or other professional services. If legal advice or other expert assistance is required, the services of a competent professional person should be sought.

Advantage Media Group is proud to be a part of the Tree Neutral® program. Tree Neutral offsets the number of trees consumed in the production and printing of this book by taking proactive steps such as planting trees in direct proportion to the number of trees used to print books. To learn more about Tree Neutral, please visit www.treeneutral.com.

Advantage Media Group is a publisher of business, self-improvement, and professional development books and online learning. We help entrepreneurs, business leaders, and professionals share their Stories, Passion, and Knowledge to help others Learn & Grow. Do you have a manuscript or book idea that you would like us to consider for publishing? Please visit **advantagefamily.com** or call **1.866.775.1696**.

This book is dedicated to everyone who has been affected by violence, evil, abuse, suicide, or other preventable tragedy. I hope this book will help you to harness the incredible power of your community's first preventers to establish a First Preventers Program in honor of those who were lost or hurt, so they are not forgotten.

CONTENTS

INTRODUCTION: WHY WRITE
THE FIRST PREVENTERS PLAYBOOK?

PART I

PREVENTION FAILURES

COMMON MYTHS ABOUT PREVENTION

A COMMUNITY OF HEROES

BARRIERS TO INTERVENTION,
DISRUPTION, AND PREVENTION

PART II

ACKNOWLEDGMENTS

I would like to thank some very special people who played important parts in the creation and evolution of not only my book from beginning to release, but also of my story and journey.

First, I would like to thank my parents for creating me and supporting me in whatever I thought I could accomplish, even when they did not fully understand my dreams. I would also like to thank my incredible and amazing daughter, who motivates me in so many ways to keep persevering and evangelizing for better prevention and to keep helping others so together we can make our communities safer.

Thank you to some close friends who listened to my ideas and helped me turn them into actions and results: Jeff Tetzlaff, Brad Ewerth, Ken Ward, Jeff Sass, Dr. Sang Lee, and Jason Destein. And thank you to many others along the way who inspired and challenged me, and even those who doubted me—that extra chip on my shoulder has been helpful.

Finally, I would like to thank some of the early adopters, truly innovative leaders, for being some of the first to implement new strategies and technologies in their organizations and communities to keep their people safe: Tenna Whitsel, Tracy Alvarez, Chief Craig Branch, Kirk Smalley, Joe Wright, and Captain Kevin Griger.

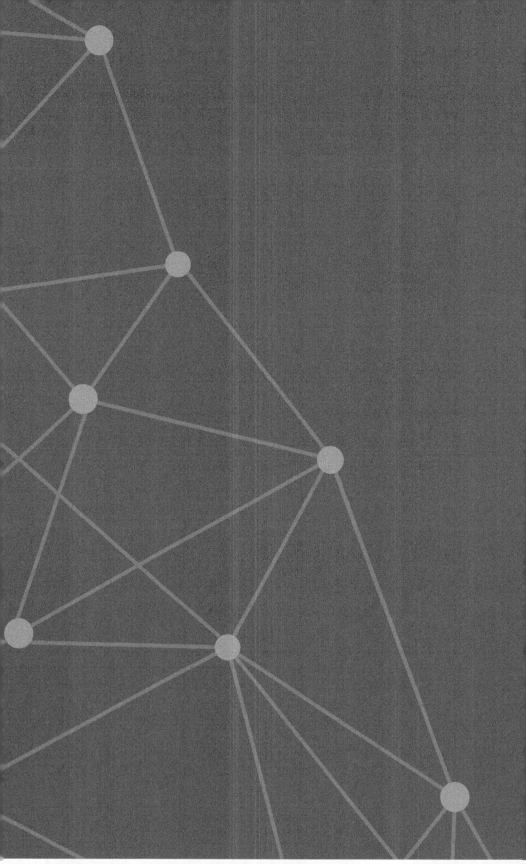

WORD FROM THE AUTHOR

My prevention career started back in the sixth grade. I was in what was called at the time a "gifted class," and our classes were held in the same building as the classes for special needs students. One of those special needs students, MJ, was constantly being bullied by other kids. As a result, she had violent and frightening seizures, after which she was left disorientated and confused. I stepped in to prevent the bullying and then recruited other kids to help. I also got the teacher involved to help stop the other kids harassing her. Eventually, these kids stopped picking on MJ, which greatly improved her life, and before long, her seizures stopped. Our collective actions were the key to preventing bullying.

For the next six years, MJ waved and smiled when she saw me. At our twenty-fifth high school reunion, she hugged me and introduced me to her husband. Since then, she has sent me multiple digital birthday cards through our reunion site.

This is what I call "return on prevention"—the positive result of proactive prevention actions that keep giving. My sixth-grade actions were my first steps as a first preventer—that is, someone who observes concerning behaviors and takes proactive actions, such as incident reporting or getting other first preventers involved in taking proactive intervention and disruption actions before an incident or a tragedy occurs.

My next return on prevention experience was as a white-hat hacker in my newly formed company, CorpNet Security. CorpNet Security became Awareity in 2003, and our services involved conducting risk and security assessments to find gaps and disconnects in organizations' online security systems. My expertise was identifying the gaps and eliminating them before black-hat hackers and cyber thieves could attack and cause problems. It became clear from our cyber assessments, research, interviews, and investigations that proactive prevention actions and ongoing information security awareness were key to stopping hackers.

During the late 1990s and the early 2000s, the Columbine massacre, the 9/11 terrorist attacks, and numerous other incidents took place even though more than enough red flags and warning signs had existed beforehand. Because of my return on prevention experiences, my passion for child safety, and my patriotism for the USA, I was motivated to find out why so many prevention efforts were failing. My research began in 2001 and was focused on the profile of failed preventions. This was different from most other research, which was focused on the profile of the attackers. My research revealed over and over how common gaps, silos, and disconnects were the reasons organizations and government agencies failed to connect the dots and prevent terrorism, violence, abuse, bullying, suicides, and numerous other incidents. However, I could not find any comprehensive solutions that focused on eliminating these common and dangerous gaps, silos, and disconnects to stop attacks that were targeting innocent children and adults in schools, organizations, and communities, so I set out to create them.

The result of my passion, my research, and my experiences led to the creation of the First Preventers Program and *The First Preventers Playbook*.

CHAPTER 1

INTRODUCTION: WHY WRITE THE FIRST PREVENTERS PLAYBOOK?

Nearly every day, we hear about school shootings, sexual assaults, workplace violence, drugs, gangs, community violence, and suicides, and for years we have been discussing incidents such as the following:

- 13 killed, April 1999, Columbine High School, Colorado

- 13 and an unborn child killed, April 2009, Fort Hood, Texas

- 17 killed, February 2018, Marjory Stoneman Douglas High School, Parkland, Florida

- 25 and an unborn killed, November 2017, First Baptist Church of Sutherland Springs, Texas

- 27 killed, December 2012, Sandy Hook Elementary School, Connecticut

- 32 killed, April 2007, Virginia Tech, Virginia

- 49 killed, June 2016, Pulse nightclub, Florida

- 58 killed, October 2017, Route 91 Harvest music festival, Las Vegas

What we don't often hear about is how these incidents and tragedies can be prevented.

Sadly, according to the US Department of Defense, 2018 was a deadlier year for American schoolchildren than for deployed service members, despite more than enough red flags and warning signs being observed and reported before the attacks occurred.[1] And 2019 had more mass shootings than days in the year.

There is no shortage of security and threat-assessment books, and most are written by people who are experts in their specific field; for example, law enforcement experts write about security and security assessments, behavioral experts write about behavioral assessments, and so on. Unfortunately, there is a lack of an overarching prevention playbook that focuses on the bigger picture and the six distinct but overlapping stages of preventing acts of violence and other incidents before they happen.

There are a lot of books offering guidelines (recipes) for threat assessment, behavior assessment, risk assessment, or security assessment, but they do not provide the comprehensive strategies, actions, and tools needed to successfully prevent more incidents and tragedies. Just having the recipe does not get the results you want. You also need the right ingredients and the right tools. This is evident because even with all the guidelines, many acts of violence are increasing. To make matters worse, bad guys and evildoers have better playbooks

---

1   Philip Bump, "2018 has been deadlier for schoolchildren than deployed service members," Washington Post, May 18, 2019, https://www.washingtonpost.com/news/politics/wp/2018/05/18/2018-has-been-deadlier-for-schoolchildren-than-service-members.

available to them on the dark web than good guys have available to them anywhere … until now.

Research presented in the following pages repeatedly shows that shootings and other acts of violence are not reduced or eliminated by maintaining the status quo in security, incident reporting, assessments, and response efforts. Despite there being more than enough warning signs observed and reported, incidents and tragedies continue. These are not limited to shootings; many suicides, sexual assaults, drug overdoses, sex abuse, school violence, and workplace violence in organizations and communities are not being prevented even though red flags are available.

The question is, How many more shootings and other acts of violence will it take before real change is made?

SCHOOL SHOOTINGS

In 1999, at Columbine High School in Colorado, two teens shot and killed thirteen people and wounded more than twenty others before turning their guns on themselves. At the time, this was the worst school shooting in US history. As of this writing, according to the *Washington Post*, there have been 230 school shootings since then.

In May 2019, Colorado experienced its fourth school shooting since Columbine when one student was killed and eight others injured at the STEM School Highlands Ranch charter school. Afterward, one teacher, who had reassured students that school was one of the safest places to be, asked, "Do they still believe me? Should they?" Parents were considering home schooling because their children didn't feel safe at school. One parent admitted, "I worry every day I kiss my kids goodbye it'll be for the last time."[2]

---

2   Ibid.

Shootings, acts of violence, and other incidents and tragedies have long-term and often horrific effects. A year after the Marjory Stoneman Douglas High School massacre in Florida, two students who were suffering from survivor's guilt committed suicide. The parent of one of the children murdered in the Sandy Hook Elementary School shooting in Connecticut, where twenty children and six adult staff members were shot, also committed suicide.

After incidents and tragedies occur, serious consequences and mounting costs can go on for years, which makes intervening, disrupting, and preventing critical.

Shortly after the Marjory Stoneman Douglas High School massacre, thousands of people took part in the March for Our Lives in Washington, DC. Similar protests were organized in other cities to show support and demand desperately needed change. One of the students said, "What we must do now is enact change because that is what we do to things that fail: We change them."[3]

Change is needed in more places than just schools. No sector has proven to be immune to the thousands of incidents and tragedies that have impacted organizations and communities for years. We have seen incidents and tragedies, not just shootings, at houses of worship, higher-education institutions, healthcare organizations, local government offices, military bases, entertainment venues, shopping malls, hospitality organizations, and numerous other places where people gather together.

Clearly a First Preventers Program is needed.

---

3   AJ Willingham, "Some of the most powerful quotes from the #NeverAgain rallies," CNN.com. February 21, 2018, https://www.cnn.com/2018/02/21/us/neveragain-parkland-shooting-rallies-quotes-trnd/index.html.

SEXUAL ABUSE

Higher education is facing an epidemic of sexual abuse involving children, students, employees, and third parties connected to higher-education institutions. The epidemic has led to hundreds of federal investigations, significant fines, expensive lawsuits, settlements amounting to hundreds of millions of dollars, institutional reputational damages, and executive leadership being fired and even going to prison.

At Ohio State University, a team doctor sexually abused at least 177 male students over nearly two decades before committing suicide. Ohio State president Michael Drake admitted there was a "consistent institutional failure" at the school.

At Harvard, after multiple allegations of sexual misconduct against a professor resurfaced, the committee responsible for scrutinizing departmental culture released a report concluding it failed to provide a safe work environment **and** called on the university to launch an independent review of "failures of communication and reporting" and the "prolonged institutional failure" that facilitated the professor's abuse.

After its failure to detect and stop sexual assaults by a sports doctor, Michigan State University was accused of a "persistent failure to take swift and decisive action to detect and stop one perpetrator's two-decade long predatory and abusive behavior [that] indicates a lack of institutional control."[4]

---

4   Michael Burke, "Education Department blasts Michigan State's handling of Nassar cases," The Hill, https://thehill.com/blogs/blog-briefing-room/news/427813-education-department-report-blasts-michigan-state-in-handling.

Changes are needed in higher education institutions to address the widespread epidemic of institutional failures caused by common gaps, silos, and disconnects.

And it is not just higher education. After being plagued by controversy, the Vatican held a summit in February 2019 with the goal of ensuring that bishops clearly understand what they need to do to prevent and combat the worldwide problem of sexual abuse of minors. "Everyone's awareness increases that abuses need to be reported to the competent authorities," the Pope said, "and for the need to cooperate with them in prevention and counteraction activities."[5]

Changes are also needed in organizations, as evinced by the spike of sexual assaults and rape reports that have emerged in the #MeToo era.

WORKPLACE VIOLENCE

Workplace violence is defined by the Occupational Safety and Health Administration (OSHA) as "any act or threat of physical violence, harassment, intimidation, or other threatening disruptive behavior that occurs at the work site." Workplace violence incidents and tragedies are the leading causes of death in the workplace. Workplace violence can occur anywhere, in nearly every sector—at military bases, universities, hospitals, manufacturing facilities, large organizations, and small organizations.

According to OSHA, nearly two million people report workplace violence each year, although it is well known that many incidents go unreported. For many years, organizations have been investing tremen-

---

5   Jason Horowitz and Elisabetta Povoledo, "Pope Issues Law, With Penalties, for Vatican City to Address Sexual Abuse," New York Times, March 29, 2019, https://www.nytimes.com/2019/03/29/world/europe/pope-sexual-abuse-law-vatican.html.

dous amounts of money, time, and resources in workplace violence policies and employee training, yet workplace violence continues to occur and even grow in some sectors. After a recent workplace shooting at a suburban Chicago place of business, the president and CEO of the parent organization said that the employee who killed five coworkers and wounded five police officers "was being terminated Friday for a culmination of various workplace rule violations."[6] He went on to say, "We're assessing if there's anything we could have done or could do in the future," adding that he was certain there were some shortcomings that would need to be addressed.

At a Venetian Resort picnic in Las Vegas, a longtime employee walked up to a table and shot two of his bosses, injuring one and killing the other. After the attack, another employee described the shooter as "just like what everyone was saying about the Parkland shooter. We all knew he was crazy. It wasn't a matter of if he would, it was when … I hate to say it, no one was surprised that he did it because he literally complained about management every single day."[7]

These two incidents offer examples of how red flags were observed and reported, but prevention efforts are still failing. They show that changes are clearly needed in workplaces to eliminate gaps between what employees know and what workplace violence teams do not know so that proactive intervention actions can be taken before employees escalate to violence.

---

6   "The Latest: CEO: Gunman passed background check when hired," Associated Press, February 16, 2019, https://www.apnews.com/61076852fb264 d3aaac62f87411066c8.

7   Carl Samson, "Disgruntled Worker Murders Las Vegas Casino Executive at Company Picnic," NextShark, April 19, 2018, https://nextshark.com/disgruntled-worker-murders-las-vegas-casino-executive-company-picnic.

NURSE AND HEALTHCARE VIOLENCE

According to OSHA, 75 percent of nearly twenty-five thousand workplace assaults reported annually occur in healthcare and social service settings,[8] but that number is grossly underreported because only about 30 percent of nurses report violent incidents. The American Nurses Association (ANA) recently launched the #EndNurseAbuse initiative to increase awareness of the serious problem of physical and verbal abuse against nurses. ANA president Dr. Pamela Cipriano said, "Abuse is not part of anyone's job and has no place in healthcare settings. Time's up for employers who don't take swift and meaningful action to make the workplace safe for nurses."[9]

Recognizing that proactive intervention, disruption, and prevention actions are needed, the Joint Commission (TJC) issued a Sentinel Event Alert in April 2018 that addressed the issue of physical and verbal violence toward nurses and healthcare workers. It stated that "healthcare organizations are encouraged to address this growing problem by looking beyond solutions that only increase security."[10] The Sentinel Event Alert also provided seven recommendations that cover actions such as incident reporting, collecting data from multiple sources, providing appropriate follow-ups, case reviews for intervention, developing quality improvement initiatives, training staff on

---

8   Lee Nelson, "Nurses Say Violent Assaults Against Healthcare Workers Are a Silent Epidemic," Nurse.org, August 12, 2019, https://nurse.org/articles/workplace-violence-in-nursing-and-hospitals.

9   Lillee Gelinas, "Workplace violence: A nurse tells her story," American Nurse Today, June 6, 2018, www.americannursetoday.com/workplace-violence-nurse-story.

10   "The Joint Commission Issues Sentinel Event Alert on Violence," Relias Media, June 1, 2018, www.reliasmedia.com/articles/142639 the joint commission issues sentinel event alert on violence.

de-escalation and self-defense, and evaluating workplace violence initiatives.

As chapter 2 will show, there is no shortage of laws, guidelines, and recommendations for how to prevent violence, but years of data and years of failures have exposed a huge problem: organizations in nearly every sector do not have the right tools, nor do they take the right actions to turn laws, guidelines, and training into the results that leaders, organizations, and communities are seeking.

GANG VIOLENCE

According to the FBI, thirty-three thousand violent street gangs, motorcycle gangs, and prison gangs are criminally active in the US today.[11] Many gangs are sophisticated and well organized, and most use violence to control neighborhoods and boost their illegal moneymaking activities. These include robbery, drug and gun trafficking, prostitution, human trafficking, and fraud. Communities often find gun violence and drug problems are closely associated with gangs. Gangs are also responsible for rising murder and homicide rates in many cities and communities across the nation.

Gang-related threats and intimidation can have a huge negative impact on the health and safety of individuals, family, peers, and community members. However, it is very difficult for law enforcement to take action against the gangs and gang members if they do not know what the community knows. In addition, people are afraid of snitching. The result is increasing levels of gang violence.

What is needed is better non–law enforcement and community-wide incident-reporting options so that people feel safe reporting red flags, concerning behaviors, violence, and other criminal and

---

11   "Gangs," FBI, www.fbi.gov/investigate/violent-crime/gangs.

noncriminal activity. An ideal and proven approach is a community-wide platform that allows people to report anonymously or confidentially using school websites, organization websites, and other non–law enforcement websites to collect the incident reports. And then, based on the incident type, notifications are automatically routed to the appropriate community-wide threat assessment team (TAT) members, who can act on the information. Creating a community-wide TAT and knowing what constitutes an effective and successful community-wide TAT will be explored in more detail in Part II of this book.

SUICIDE

Suicide is currently the second-leading cause of death among individuals between the ages of ten and thirty-four, and it is the fourth-leading cause of death among individuals between the ages of thirty-five and fifty-four. There were more than twice as many suicides (47,173) in the US as there were homicides (19,510) in 2017.[12] Suicides are a major public health problem that impacts many people, in some cases leading to copycat suicides and suicide attempts.[13]

Active duty military suicides hit a record high in 2018, and suicides among law enforcement and veterans have increased over the last decade.[14] The following table shows the loss of lives due to suicides,

---

12 "Suicide," National Institute of Mental Health, https://www.nimh.nih.gov/health/statistics/suicide.

13 Margot Sanger-Katz, "The Science Behind Suicide Contagion," The New York Times, August 13, 2014, https://www.nytimes.com/2014/08/14/upshot/the-science-behind-suicide-contagion.

14 Patricia Kime, "Active-Duty Military Suicides at Record Highs in 2018," Military.com, January 30, 2019, https://www.military.com/daily-news/2019/01/30/active-duty-military-suicides-near-record-highs-2018.html.

drug overdoses, homicides, and mass shootings. These numbers show that while the media focuses on active shooters, other incidents and tragedies have a substantial cost to human life. It is important therefore to take a broader view of the threats and challenges that exist and require a change in efforts to intervene, prevent, and disrupt them.

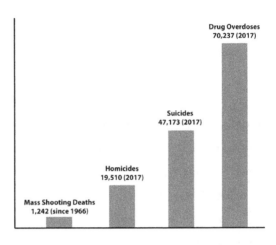

Changes are needed so that anyone who is demonstrating warning signs or suicidal behaviors and/or struggling with suicidal ideation can be identified and helped before the situation escalates and the individual attempts suicide.

VALIDATION FOR CHANGE

In its 2018 School Security Guide, the Department of Homeland Security (DHS) wrote,

> DHS recognizes that physical protection measures only go so far when it comes to preventing an active shooter incident. Social issues such as mental health, bullying, and criminal profiling play a critical role in the prevention of gun violence in schools. Potential warning signs are not always the result of a direct threat—More often, there is observable conduct which sends up a red flag, so to speak. The importance of detecting and addressing concerning behavior, thoughts, or statements cannot be overstated. In fact, preventing violence

by detecting and addressing these red flags is more effective than any physical security measure.[15]

This statement is a powerful validation of the need for change because it makes it clear that adding more security measures is not effective. This DHS statement emphasizes that the most effective way to prevent more incidents and tragedies is to focus on detecting and addressing red flags, concerning behaviors, and other warning signs.

Studies from the FBI and the US Secret Service have also validated that red flags and warning signs were almost always observed and/or leaked before incidents and tragedies occurred. Studies like these make it clear that intervention, disruption, and prevention should be possible more often. Unfortunately, most schools, universities, organizations, communities, and state and federal government offices still turn to security measures as the primary solution instead of developing the role of first preventers in a community-wide program that facilitates the reporting of red flags and warning signs that in turn become actionable information for community-wide first preventers.

WHO ARE FIRST PREVENTERS AND FIRST RESPONDERS?

Most people know that first responders include law enforcement, emergency response, EMTs, firefighters, security, and resource officers. First responders are involved in nearly every incident, massacre, and tragedy in communities and across the nation as a whole. First responders are heroes, and they respond immediately no matter the situation.

---

15   "K-12 School Security," 2nd ed., Department of Homeland Security, 2018, https://www.cisa.gov/sites/default/files/publications/K12-School-Security-Guide-2nd-Edition-508.pdf.

First preventers, on the other hand, include students, employees, family, friends, neighbors, social media users, TAT members, mental health experts, social workers, and everyone else who might have information about a possible perpetrator. First preventers have the potential to become part of a team of heroes by observing and reporting red flags and suspicious activities. From there, the TAT can assess the red flags and at-risk individuals, connect the dots, and collaborate with other resources to effectively intervene, monitor, and undertake ongoing prevention efforts.

First preventers, as part of an effective First Preventers Program that utilizes *The First Preventers Playbook*, are critically needed to complement first responders. The essential components of an effective First Preventers Program will be presented in Part II.

WHY WRITE THE FIRST PREVENTERS PLAYBOOK?

Better prevention is needed, and research reveals better prevention is possible, but most organizations and communities do not have a First Preventers Program to complement their first responders. Leaders in schools, higher education, organizations, and communities are beginning to ask how to prevent incidents and tragedies, and they're beginning to look for new prevention solutions, so understanding how to implement the First Preventers Program is key to leading the way. Without a playbook, leaders and their organizations and communities will continue to struggle to prevent because gaps, silos, and disconnects still exist, which means that red flags continue to be scattered, not assessed, not connected, and not acted on. It is imperative, therefore, that executives and threat-assessment teams know how to more effectively eliminate gaps, silos, and disconnects to more effectively intervene, disrupt, and prevent.

By educating, empowering, and equipping first preventers to collect, assess, and connect the dots and take the right actions to disrupt at-risk individuals on the pathway to violence, more violent incidents and tragedies can be prevented, and fewer first responders will have to put their lives on the line.

This is where *The First Preventers Playbook* comes in. *The First Preventers Playbook* is the result of decades of extensive and ongoing research conducted since 2001 into hundreds of post-incident reports. In the following chapters, *The First Preventers Playbook* provides a play-by-play for executive management team members who are responsible for establishing effective prevention and who are concerned with improving safety for schools, organizations, and communities.

Part I examines why people do not know how to collect and connect the dots. It's partly due to barriers, partly due to myths surrounding incident reporting, and partly due to a lack of understanding of the common and preventable failures that lead up to every incident and tragedy. Part I presents cases of real-life incidents and profiles of failed preventions as well as common barriers to prevention. It addresses and identifies common gaps, silos, and disconnects in the collecting, assessing, connecting, intervening, preventing, and ongoing awareness stages of prevention. It offers examples of the gaps, silos, and disconnects that precede shootings and other incidents and tragedies.

Part II looks at what constitutes the First Preventers Program. It outlines who first preventers are and what they can do. It presents proven research-based approaches for different incidents to show people how to take action when faced with different potential risks. Based on information acquired from the analysis of post-incident reports, it also presents comprehensive research and proven solutions to help organizations and communities learn how to take action to intervene, disrupt, and prevent shootings and other violent incidents, suicides, and tragedies.

Part II also introduces the First Preventers Platform, a key component of any First Preventers Program, which makes it possible for anyone anywhere to confidentially or anonymously report suspicious activity, red flags, and warning signs; collect warning signs from other silo incident-reporting systems; automatically route notifications of incident reports to all the right team members; provide tools for team members to assess, investigate, assign tasks, connect with related information, and connect with appropriate resources for intervention and monitoring; and take immediate actions to prevent escalations and incidents. The platform also provides tools for advanced data analytics to identify patterns and trends and improve proactive and preventive actions to address them. The First Preventers Platform empowers first preventers and TAT members in organizations and communities to act proactively and prevent rather than just react and respond.

Finally, Part II provides a guide for executive management responsible for setting up TATs and policies and procedures for the TAT members themselves as well as for other organizations and community leaders concerned with improving safety for schools and communities.

In short, the following chapters will lay out powerful and effective solutions to empower all first preventers by focusing on proven strategies. With this guide, more incidents and tragedies can be prevented before the need to call first responders even arises.

PART I

WHAT IS PREVENTION?

Prevention, in essence, refers to stopping a violent incident or other tragedy before it happens.

Psychologists, behavior specialists, and numerous others agree that there is a pathway to violence that usually escalates over a period of time, which means there is time to intervene and disrupt it. In other words, the pathway to violence is a pathway to prevention.

Unfortunately, too often, prevention efforts fail. For a number of reasons, at-risk individuals fall through the cracks and succeed in perpetrating acts of violence or acts of evil on innocent people. This part of the book examines what tools, systems, people, information, and resources are needed for effective prevention; what are common prevention myths; and what barriers exist to effective intervention, disruption, and prevention.

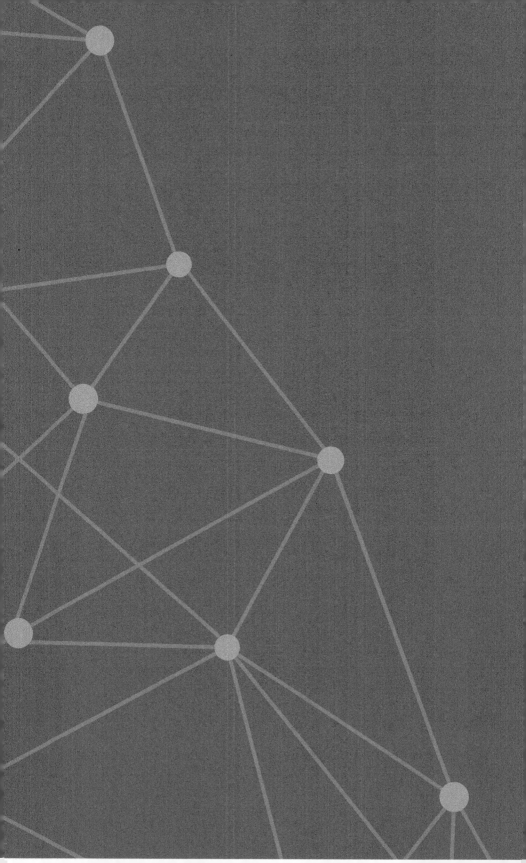

CHAPTER 2

PREVENTION FAILURES

In the Columbine High School massacre in 1999, twelve students and one teacher were killed before the attackers turned the guns on themselves. Three months later, twelve people were killed in a shooting in Georgia. That fall, seven were killed in the Wedgwood Baptist Church shooting in Fort Worth, Texas. In November, another seven people were killed in the Xerox killings in Honolulu. In December, five people were killed in the Tampa Hotel shootings in Florida. The following year, seven more were killed at the Wakefield massacre in Massachusetts, and two years after that, six people were killed in the Lockheed Martin shooting in Mississippi. Then, of course, there was the 9/11 attack, in which 2,977 people were killed.

The 9/11 Commission Report said authorities failed to connect the dots; similarly, post-incident reports for almost every attack since 1999 showed that red flags and warning signs existed but were not collected, not connected, and not acted upon.

COLUMBINE, PARKLAND, AND 9/11

The 570-page, 14-chapter 9/11 Commission Report concluded that a "failure of imagination" kept US officials from understanding the al Qaeda threat before the attacks on New York and Washington.[16] It identified significant warning signs that dated back to 1994, including the hijacking of an Air France plane in 1998, the memo of an FBI agent highlighting a number of Arab men seeking flight training in Oklahoma City that was not sent to FBI headquarters, an FAA warning to airlines and airports to maintain a "high degree of alertness" in response to statements made by Osama bin Laden in the aftermath of the US bombings of al Qaeda targets in Afghanistan and Sudan, and an FAA warning of the possibility of a hijacking at an eastern US airport. In 1999, the media announced that a report commissioned by the National Intelligence Council stated that al Qaeda posed the most serious terrorist threat to US security interests and warned that it "could crash-land an aircraft packed with high explosives (C-4 and Semtex) into the Pentagon, CIA headquarters, or the White House."[17] In January 2000, the CIA tracked one hijacker to Los Angeles but did not alert the Immigration and Naturalization Service or FBI of his entry into the US. In September that year, US intelligence began to intercept chatter about a series of threats against the country.

Between January and September 11, 2001, the FAA issued fifteen information circulars containing generalized warnings about terrorist threats and hijackings. That spring, four defendants stood trial in New

---

16   "September 11 Warning Signs Fast Facts," CNN.com, August 23, 2019, https://www.cnn.com/2013/07/27/us/september-11th-warning-signs-fast-facts/index.html.

17   Gwyneth K. Shaw and Tamara Lytle, "CIA advisers got warning 2 1/2 years ago," The Orlando Sentinel, May 18, 2001, https://www.orlandosentinel.com/news/os-xpm-2002-05-18-0205180344-story.html

York for the 1998 embassy bombings. Prosecution witnesses described buying airplanes and learning to fly them at the request of bin Laden. In the summer of 2001, the FAA issued a warning about a threat to use explosives in an airport terminal. A second warning was issued to airlines advising them that "terror groups are known to be planning and training for hijackings." In August, CIA Director George Tenet became concerned that an al Qaeda attack was imminent and sent an urgent cable to the FBI, State Department, Customs, and INS, alerting them to the CIA's concerns about two of the attackers, who had entered the US only weeks before. On September 10, the National Security Agency intercepted two communications from Afghanistan to Saudi Arabia. One said, "Tomorrow is zero hour," and the other said, "The match begins tomorrow." The messages were not translated until September 12.

As a result of this uncoordinated, disconnected, siloed, unfocused intelligence failure, the 9/11 Commission Report called for a single national intelligence chief and counterterrorism center and the creation of a single, joint congressional committee to oversee homeland security.

This recommendation to create a centralized approach to eliminate gaps, silos, and disconnects involving federal and law enforcement agencies has helped. However, the attackers and terrorists adapted too, and now a centralized and proactive first preventers approach is needed at the community level to make communities safer.

Silos of Information BEFORE the Columbine High School Shooting

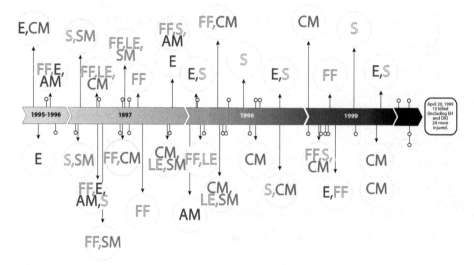

Figure 1. Timeline of Columbine

The puzzle pieces (Fig. 1) of the timeline leading up to the Columbine massacre show the extent of the warning signs that were observed and available before the attack on the school. The two shooters made comments to fellow students, who then voiced their concerns. They leaked videos of their target practice, which included comments about shooting people. In other words, they leaked what they were going to do beforehand. The school counselor who had been seeing one shooter for depression knew he had suicidal thoughts. Teachers noticed behavior and personality changes. They also noticed the shooters had started wearing Goth clothes and long black coats. Other students later reported knowing the shooters were up to something. Unfortunately, the post-incident analysis showed there were so many information gaps and other disconnects that a more complete picture of the escalation was not seen before the event in order for appropriate intervention and prevention actions to be taken.

Putting these red flags and warning signs into a timeline shows why a central community-wide platform was needed to collect, organize, and share this information instead of being siloed across multiple departments and individuals. A comprehensive platform solution and prevention program that went far beyond incident reporting was needed.

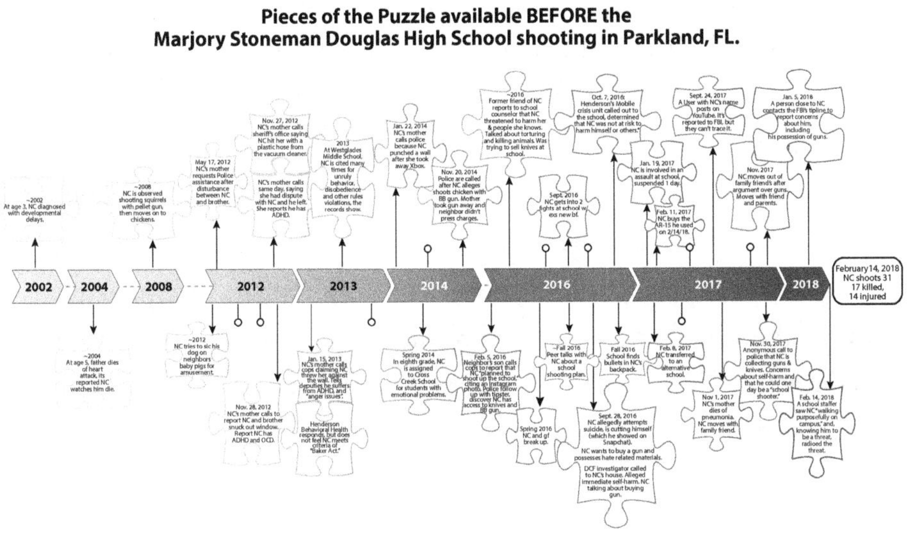

Pieces of the Puzzle available BEFORE the Marjory Stoneman Douglas High School shooting in Parkland, FL.

Timeline years: 2002 – 2004 – 2008 – 2012 – 2013 – 2014 – 2016 – 2017 – 2018 – February 14, 2018 NC shoots 31, 17 killed, 14 injured

Timeline entries:

- ~2002 At age 3, NC diagnosed with developmental delays.
- ~2004 At age 5, father dies of heart attack, its reported NC watches him die.
- ~2008 NC is observed shooting squirrels with pellet gun, then moves on to chickens.
- ~2012 NC tries to sic his dog on neighbors' dog on neighbors' baby pigs for amusement.
- May 17, 2012 NC's mother requests Police assistance after disturbance between NC and brother.
- Nov. 27, 2012 NC's mother calls sheriff's office saying NC hit her with a plastic hose from the vacuum cleaner.
- Nov. 28, 2012 NC's mother calls to report NC and brother snuck out window. Report NC has ADHD and OCD.
- Jan. 15, 2013 NC's mother calls cops claiming NC threw her against the wall. They request he follow through from ADHD and "anger issues."
- Henderson Behavioral Health responds, but does not feel NC meets criteria of "Baker Act."
- 2013 At Westglades Middle School, NC is cited many times for unruly behavior, disobedience and other rules violations, the records show.
- NC's mother calls same day, saying she had dispute with NC and he left. She reports he has ADHD.
- Jan. 23, 2014 NC's mother calls police because NC punched a wall after she took away Xbox.
- Spring 2014 In eighth grade, NC is assigned to Cross Creek School for students with emotional problems.
- Nov. 20, 2014 Police are called after NC alleges shoots chicken with BB gun. Mother took gun away and neighbor didn't press charges.
- ~2010 Former friend of NC reports to school counselor that NC threatened to harm her & people she knows. Talked about torturing and killing animals. Was trying to sell knives at school.
- Feb. 5, 2016 Neighbor's son calls cops to report that NC "planned to shoot up the school" citing an Instagram photo. Police follow up with tipster, discover NC has access to knives and BB gun.
- Spring 2016 NC and gf break up.
- Sept. 2016 NC gets into 2 fights at school and has new bf.
- Sept. 28, 2016 NC allegedly attempts suicide, is cutting himself (which he showed on Snapchat).
- ~Fall 2016 Peer talks with NC about a school shooting plan.
- Fall 2016 School finds bullets in NC's backpack.
- Oct. 7, 2016 Henderson's Mobile crisis unit called out to the school, determined that NC was not at risk to harm himself or others.
- DCF investigator called to NC's house. Alleged immediate self-harm, NC talking about buying gun.
- Jan. 19, 2017 NC is involved in an assault at school, suspended 1 day.
- Feb. 8, 2017 NC transferred to an alternative school.
- Feb. 11, 2017 NC buys the AR-15 he used on 2/14/18.
- Sept. 24, 2017 A User with NC's name posts on YouTube. It's reported to FBI, but they can't trace it.
- Nov. 1, 2017 NC's mother dies of pneumonia. NC moves with family friend.
- Nov. 2017 NC moves out of family friend's after argument over guns. Moves with friend and parents.
- Nov. 30, 2017 Anonymous call to police that NC is collecting guns & knives. Concerns about self-harm and that he could one day be a "school shooter."
- Jan. 5, 2018 A person close to NC contacts the FBI tipline to report concerns about him, including his possession of guns.
- NC wants to buy a gun and possesses hate-related materials.
- Feb. 14, 2018 A school staffer saw NC "walking purposefully on campus" and, knowing him to be a threat, radioed the threat.

Figure 2. Timeline of Parkland

In 2018, almost twenty years after the Columbine massacre, an even deadlier attack happened at Marjory Stoneman Douglas High School in Parkland, Florida, where seventeen students and staff members were killed. In the post-incident analysis, it emerged that the shooter had been expelled in 2017 for behavioral problems. Child Protective Services knew he had a troubled home life. During 2016 and 2017, the sheriff's office received a number of tips about the shooter's threats to carry out a school shooting. He even posted a YouTube video about becoming a school shooter. In 2018, the FBI tip line received a complaint that the shooter had made a death threat, but it was not forwarded to the local FBI office.[18] According to CNN, which obtained the sheriff's office log, forty-five calls were made about the shooter, his brother, or problems at the family home. One of these even reported that the shooter had threatened to shoot up the school. A month before the shooting, the FBI's See Something, Say Something line received a tip from a person who was close to the shooter, saying that he was exhibiting erratic behavior and had the means and desire to kill people. The FBI conducted an investigation, but its findings were not forwarded to the Miami field office, where investigative steps could have been taken.[19]

In summary, law enforcement had been to the shooter's house over thirty times, but the school's TAT did not know about these red flags and pre-incident indicators. Law enforcement did not know what the school knew. Law enforcement had some information, the community had other information, and the school had yet other pieces of information, but there was no central community-wide way to collect and connect this information from the different silos and bring it together so that the bigger picture of the threats and red flags could be assessed and acted on. Gaps, silos, and disconnects can be very dangerous.

---

18   Katie Benner, Patricia Mazzei, and Adam Goldman, "F.B.I. Was Warned of Florida Suspect's Desire to Kill but Did Not Act," The New York Times, February 16, 2018, https://www.nytimes.com/2018/02/16/us/fbi-nikolas-cruz-shooting.html.

19   Curt Devine and Jose Pagliery, "Sheriff says he got 23 calls about shooter's family, but records show more," CNN, February 27, 2018, https://www.cnn.com/2018/02/27/us/parkland-shooter-cruz-sheriff-calls-invs/index.html.

REACTIVE VS. PROACTIVE PREVENTION

Reactive prevention involves elements such as security cameras, alarms, panic buttons, security guards, locks, and window film. All these security measures react to an attacker or threat that is already at the front door. Alarms go off, guards come running, the automatic locks start locking, and panic buttons are hit. First responders *are called to respond to an attack in progress*. Reactive and response actions such as these are not proactive prevention actions.

SECURITY VS. PROACTIVE PREVENTION

Fort Hood has experienced two shootings, one in 2009 and the other in 2014. In 2009, an army major killed thirteen people and injured thirty. In 2014, four were killed and fourteen injured by an army specialist who then shot himself. Fort Hood has more security than most any school or organization could afford or maintain, but it still experienced two shootings.

Clearly, preventing attacks and violence is not just about how much security an organization can afford. Preventing is about empowering first preventers to collect and connect the dots and intervene *before* the at-risk individuals are allowed to escalate and before first responders have to put themselves in harm's way.

LAW ENFORCEMENT AND PROACTIVE PREVENTION

Most people have been told to call law enforcement or the FBI's See Something, Say Something when they notice suspicious activities. However, law enforcement actions are limited with suspicious activities if a crime has not been committed. All too often people say after the fact, "I called law enforcement, but it seems like they didn't do anything." Unfortunately, the next time people see a red flag or warning sign, they may not call because the last time they called, nothing was done. This misunderstanding contributes to a growing trust gap between the public and law enforcement. This is another reason the First Preventers Program is needed—to collect suspicious activities and red flags and connect them with first preventers on a community-wide TAT so that proactive prevention actions can be taken sooner rather than later when the crime occurs.

SECURITY MEASURES AND PROACTIVE PREVENTION

As mentioned earlier, DHS has stated that "preventing violence by detecting and addressing these red flags is more effective than any physical measure." The key to successful and proactive prevention, therefore, is in giving first preventers and TAT members the means to collect, assess, and connect the dots and take proactive actions. This requires strategic and comprehensive information flow originating from trusted community collection points, followed by notifications and secure information sharing with the right team members who can do the right things, right away. We will look at the mechanism that allows this information to flow in more detail in Part II.

> The key to successful and proactive prevention, therefore, is in giving first preventers and TAT members the means to collect, assess, and connect the dots and take proactive actions.

A NEW SOLUTION

Nearly every organization faces gaps, silos, and disconnects similar to those faced by Columbine and Parkland and hundreds of others. However, as attacks continue, it has become clear that a new solution that focuses on identifying hundreds of gaps, silos, and disconnects and creating strategies and the right tools to eliminate them is urgently needed.

Like a surgical team, SWAT team, or sports team, every team must have the right tools to be effective. When it comes to prevention, a central comprehensive platform with the right tools that collects, shares, and connects all available information from private citizens, school kids, teachers, employees, law enforcement, incident-reporting systems, department systems, multiple organizations, and local government agencies is key to more effective preventing. The platform of tools must be simple to use and allow people to communicate effectively. The tools must allow the TAT to share information securely across silos and collaborate with internal and external resources to ensure gaps on the path to prevention are eliminated.

In 2009, Awareity began its undertaking of this task to create a new solution. Gaps, silos, and disconnects exposed in hundreds of incidents were analyzed, and tools to eliminate each were created. It took several years to analyze the research and develop an organization-wide and community-wide solution.

In 2012, Awareity's first school-wide and community-wide web-based platform was implemented by a school in Oklahoma. In the first two weeks, the platform solved a previous incident that school security and local law enforcement had not been able to solve. Students had not wanted to talk directly to school security or law enforcement, but when they learned a new web-based platform would allow them to report information anonymously, incident reports came in, and the TAT members from the school had the information they needed to solve the incident. Just as importantly, a clear message was sent to those who were thinking about attacking others: they could no longer hope the fear of snitching would protect them from consequences.

In the first year at the Oklahoma school, the new platform was key to disrupting an active shooter escalation when multiple incident reports were received on the web-based community-wide platform regarding a student who was displaying concerning behaviors and red flags. Rather than being siloed by conventional old-school approaches, the platform empowered students, faculty, staff, parents, and TAT members to work together as first preventers to intervene, disrupt, and prevent the attack and numerous other escalations.

THE BUTTERFLY EFFECT—A NEW SOLUTION FOR SNITCHING

The idea of the butterfly effect came about at the 139th meeting of the American Association for the Advancement of Science forty-five years ago. During the meeting, chaos theory mathematician Edward Lorenz asked if the flap of a butterfly's wings in Brazil would set off a tornado in Texas. Lorenz had observed the complexity of interdependent cause-and-effect relationships.[20]

> A very small change in initial conditions can create a significantly different outcome.

Today the butterfly effect theory is associated with the idea that small actions can have profound and widely divergent effects on outcomes.

---

20 Jamie L. Vernon, "Understanding the Butterfly Effect," American Scientist, https://www.americanscientist.org/article/understanding-the-butterfly-effect.

In other words, a very small change in initial conditions can create a significantly different outcome. [21] The butterfly effect theory seemed appropriate to utilize incident reports, no matter how small the red flag might seem, to achieve significantly better prevention results. The First Preventers Platform created the unique butterfly effect icon to become a recognizable symbol that is synonymous with confidential and/or anonymous incident reporting for any suspicious behavior or red flag that someone observed.

Clicking on the butterfly icon puts the butterfly effect into action, in that a single report of a red flag, concerning behavior, suspicious activity, or social media comment could be the piece of the puzzle that saves lives, reputations, and bottom lines and changes the world forever for many people who might have been involved in an attack or incident. In other words, clicking the butterfly icon makes everyone a first preventer who can initiate proactive prevention efforts. And because the butterfly effect is about how an incident report could save a life, a friend, a colleague, a family member, and so on, the butterfly icon helps eliminate the fear of snitching because now first preventers are helping, not snitching.

The butterfly icon also provides a safe and trusted option for first preventers to use instead of calling law enforcement, which could also be perceived as snitching, and then the information does not get shared—although it could be the piece of the puzzle that TAT members need.

---

21   Edward N. Lorenz, "Deterministic Nonperiodic Flow," Journal of the Atmospheric Sciences 20, no. 2 (March 1963): 130–141.

LAST WORD

The more information that is collected and shared, the clearer the picture is and the more likely the right people can take the right actions.

For example, within the first seventy days of rolling out the platform as part of a countywide solution, Sarpy County, Nebraska, received over one hundred incident reports with new pieces of information relating to at-risk individuals who might pose potential harm to others or to themselves as suicide risks. The Sarpy County TAT members then reviewed the information collected on the secure, central, countywide platform and were able to connect the dots and assess what course of action to take to disrupt issues instead of waiting for them to happen.[22]

As Sarpy County proves, the key to successfully disrupting and preventing an attack lies in making sure everyone in the community can simply access one of multiple websites, click on the icon, and report anything suspicious.

Ultimately, overcoming and eliminating the fear of snitching, eliminating frustrations that previous incident reports have resulted in no action, giving people non–law enforcement options to share information, and using the butterfly icon and the butterfly effect have proven to be successful and the way of the future.

---

22   Holly Gilbert Stowell, "The Power of Awareness," Security Management, April 1, 2019, https://www.asisonline. org/security-management-magazine/articles/2019/04/ the-power-of-awareness.

CHAPTER 3

COMMON MYTHS ABOUT PREVENTION

One of the most common myths about security is that incidents and tragedies can be prevented with more armed guards, more locks, more cameras, and more security measures. Adding more security measures is a common response after almost every shooting, violent incident, and tragedy. Unfortunately, adding more security measures has not proven to be an effective way to prevent and reduce incidents and tragedies from occurring, especially with at-risk individuals who are undeterred by security measures.

In 2013, the Washington Navy Yard was attacked, leaving twelve dead and three more injured, despite this being the headquarters of the US Naval Sea Systems Command (NAVSEA). Virginia Tech had its own campus police force, but in the massacre there in 2007, thirty-two people were killed and seventeen wounded. In 2015, fourteen people were killed and twenty-two others were seriously injured in a mass shooting and an attempted bombing of a government building in San Bernardino, California. **The city of San Bernardino has its own police force.** As mentioned earlier, the Texas military base at

31

Fort Hood has more security, armed guards, cameras, alarms, access controls, security gates, and technology than most any school, college, or organization, but this security did not stop the deadliest shooting on a US army base from happening in 2009 and a second attack five years later or shootings at the Naval Air Station in Pensacola or the Naval Station Pearl Harbor.

Security measures work well in prisons. However, in an open environment, such as a school or a college or a business where people come and go, security measures are limited and not as effective. Adding more security to a school just makes it look like a prison, which nobody wants.

Security is necessary, and security measures can be a good deterrent for some, but security alone is not effective with the undeterred, and security is not designed to deliver intervention, disruption, and prevention. This chapter presents and explores three common security-related myths.

MYTH 1: SECURITY CAMERAS PREVENT ATTACKS

Security cameras are good at recording what happened and providing forensic evidence, but they do not prevent attackers from attacking. In fact, many attackers planned on being recorded on camera so they would gain attention and notoriety in the news and on social media.

In addition, 95 percent or more of security cameras are not monitored in real time. On high-tech military bases, security cameras may be monitored around the clock, but this is generally not the case in most organizations, which lack the resources to monitor them 24/7. Parkland had a security camera feed going to law enforcement, but the security camera feed had a twenty-minute delay. Unfortunately, law enforcement did not realize there was a delay, and by the time they mobilized, the shooter had already left the school and gone to a local restaurant for a soda.

Because of the lack of resources, many organizations outsource security

> Even with billions being spent on security, incidents and attacks are still occurring and even increasing.

camera monitoring. In schools, higher-education institutions, businesses, and homes across the country, billions of dollars are spent on security cameras, alarms, access controls, panic buttons, and monitoring. The physical security market is projected to grow from $84.1 billion in 2018 to $119.4 billion by 2023.[23] However, even with billions being spent on security, incidents and attacks are still occurring and even increasing.

			REACTIVE Measures						PREVENTIVE Measures
Year	Incident Name	Type	Cameras	Locks	Security Systems	Guards/ Police	Access Control	Red Flags	First Preventers Program/ Connecting the Dots Platform
1999	Columbine High School	Shooting	YES	YES	YES	YES	YES	YES	NO
2007	Virginia Tech	Shooting	YES	YES	YES	YES	YES	YES	NO
2009	Fort Hood	Terrorism	YES	YES	YES	YES	YES	YES	NO
2012	Sandy Hook Elementary	Shooting	YES	YES	YES	YES	YES	YES	NO
2014	Isla Vista/ UC Santa Barbara	Shooting	YES	YES	YES	YES	YES	YES	NO
2014	Fort Hood	Terrorism	YES	YES	YES	YES	YES	YES	NO
2015	San Bernardino	Terrorism	YES	YES	YES	YES	YES	YES	NO
2018	Marjory Stoneman Douglas High School	Shooting	YES	YES	YES	YES	YES	YES	NO
2019	Naval Air Pensacola	Terrorism	YES	YES	YES	YES	YES	YES	NO
2019	Virginia Beach Municipal	Shooting	YES	YES	YES	YES	YES	YES	NO
2020	Milwaukee Coors Brewery	Shooting	YES	YES	YES	YES	YES	YES	NO

23   "Physical Security Market," Markets and Markets, August 2019, https:// www.marketsandmarkets.com/Market-Reports/physical-security-market-1014.html.

MYTH 2: SEE SOMETHING, SAY SOMETHING

Months after the terrorist attacks on September 11, 2001, advertising executive and entrepreneur Allen Kay came up with the slogan "See Something, Say Something" to encourage public transportation riders to join New York's Metropolitan Transportation Authority security efforts by reporting warning signs. The campaign saw the reporting of suspicious packages increase from 814 in 2002 to over 37,000 in 2003.[24]

While the initial response to the campaign was impressive, incident reports are now decreasing, and silo-related challenges are increasing. One such silo-related challenge is that tips are reported to a law enforcement hotline or website and from there go into a federal, state, or local law enforcement database. This law enforcement information is rarely shared with individual organizations in the community that have additional red flags and pieces of the puzzle, and the result is siloed information. In addition, law enforcement usually doesn't have the resources to respond to or track and monitor a person acting suspiciously, and in many cases, it is not legally permitted to do so if no crime has been committed. Law enforcement must also be careful to avoid profiling, invasion of privacy, and violating an individual's civil rights.

Law enforcement officers are first responders, and their expertise is in responding to incidents and crimes that have been committed, so suspicious activities may not be a high priority compared to other calls they receive.

---

24   Annie Karni, "The MTA Has a Message for Television Watchers," The Sun, Jul 18, 2007, https://www.nysun.com/new-york/mta-has-a-message-for-television-watchers/58616/.

As previously mentioned, a serious and widening gap with See Something, Say Something arises from distrust of law enforcement and because people report nonemergency or suspicious activity and nothing happens. A snowball effect ensues when people do not see action being taken. They stop calling, and future warning signs are not reported. This increases the likelihood that prevention efforts will fail. Unfortunately, the widening trust gap between community members and law enforcement keeps people from calling to report suspicious activities, red flags, or warning signs.

Because of these serious and widening gaps, new first preventer strategies and complementary options to See Something, Say Something are clearly and immediately needed so as much information as possible is collected and utilized rather than being scattered across the community or the nation.

MYTH 3: LAWS PREVENT CRIMES

Laws have been around for as long as there have been societies. In fact, there has been a law against homicide in the US since 1790,[25] but murders are committed every day, which clearly shows having laws by itself does not prevent homicides.

Hundreds of laws have been created to prevent violence, sexual assaults, bullying, human trafficking, drug trafficking, child abuse, and numerous other incidents and attacks. However, only the good guys follow the laws, while it is clear that most bad guys and evildoers are undeterred by laws and ignore them.

Many laws are created to define penalties. However, suicide bombers, murder-suicide attackers, and most mass shooters do not

---

25   The Public Statutes at Large for the United States of America, An Act for the Punishment of Certain Crimes against the United States, pp. 112–113.

care about penalties; therefore, the laws do not deter or prevent them from attacking.

For these reasons and numerous others, laws alone should not be considered an effective solution for preventing terrorists, evildoers, and other bad guys from attacking and abusing others.

LAST WORD

Security measures; See Something, Say Something; law enforcement; and laws are all important response solutions. However, they are not proving to be effective in deterring and preventing attacks, incidents, and tragedies before they occur.

Relying on security-related measures has allowed way too many tragic consequences to occur. What can be done as more and more people are saying enough is enough and asking how to prevent? The next chapter examines some positive developments in communities coming together for proactive prevention.

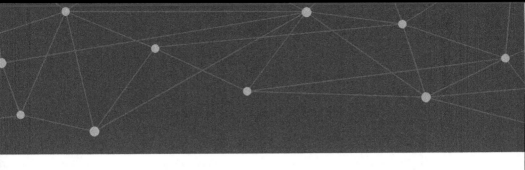

CHAPTER 4

A COMMUNITY OF HEROES

Successful sports teams need both defense and offense to be effective. Take football, for example. If a football team only had defense and the defense had to play the full game, then no matter how good the defense was, that team would not win very many games. The successful teams that come out on top have a good offense and a good defense.

The same holds true in a community of heroes. To make sure an organization and a community are successful, both first responders and first preventers are needed.

> The successful teams that come out on top have a good offense and a good defense.

ONE TEAM OF HEROES

Every day, first responders put their lives on the line when they respond to violence, crimes, and numerous other incidents. They storm into the middle of an attack to take down shooters, stop violence, and evacuate people caught up in incidents. They deal with gangs, drugs, suicides, and numerous other incidents. It is a dangerous job that can have long-term repercussions and costly consequences. Many states are passing laws to set aside millions of dollars to help first responders deal with PTSD and other related challenges, as many first responders have developed ongoing physical and mental health issues from 9/11 and numerous other tragedies.

What if the First Preventers Program could help to interrupt, disrupt, and prevent more at-risk individuals and situations from escalating into incidents and tragedies? This could reduce the number of incidents that require first responders to put their lives on the line, reduce long-term repercussions, reduce future PTSD challenges, and help states save millions of dollars.

Everyone recognizes first responders as heroes, but first preventers can be heroes too. They are the people who could report the red flags and suspicious activities so intervention can take place before a situation escalates. For example, the bus driver in the Santa Fe shooting in 2018, in which ten people were killed and thirteen more injured, could have been a first preventer when, knowing the seventeen-year-old shooter didn't play any sport, he saw him bring a big sports bag onto the bus. What if the driver had been equipped to report the red flag? What if an automatic and immediate notification had alerted one of Santa Fe's eight sworn officers or TAT members who were on duty the day of the shooting to check out the bag?

The neighbors in San Bernardino in 2015 who observed suspicious activities taking place over a period of time were potential first preventers, but they didn't feel comfortable coming forward to law enforcement so no TAT members were made aware before the attackers took the lives of fourteen people and injured twenty-two in a mass shooting and an attempted bombing at the Inland Regional Center.

Too often today, organizations and communities depend almost entirely on first responders. This means they are depending on the defense to avert an attack and thus keep the organization and community safe. However, saving lives and saving future costs depends on a good offense—that is, the first preventers, who have the means to take immediate actions to identify red flags, intervene with at-risk individuals, and disrupt and prevent incidents and tragedies from happening. No matter how fast the first responders are on-site, horrific and tragic damages can still occur.

As mentioned previously, most post-incident reports show there were many warning signs about at-risk individuals who escalated and executed acts of violence and evil. What is needed, therefore, is a community-wide team consisting of **first responders and first preventers who can, with the right tools and strategies, work together to effectively disrupt, intervene, and prevent attacks before they happen.**

ANATOMY OF A COMMUNITY-WIDE TEAM: SARPY COUNTY

Captain Kevin Griger of the Sarpy County *Sheriff's* Office in Nebraska is a trailblazer in community-wide team building. He had a great defense—that is, a first responder team of law enforcement, EMTs, social workers, and crisis response teams—but he did not have the right strategies and the right tools to quickly get information out of silos, to eliminate gaps and disconnects, and to automatically connect the dots with the right intervention and prevention team members. This was due to limited resources, too many sparsely attended meetings, silo systems, silo organizations, and a lack of secure information sharing. He knew he had gaps, but he did not know how to eliminate them. He was also working with four separate school districts to help prevent suicides, sexual assaults, violence, and numerous other incident types.

Even though he had a great defense, he needed to proactively prevent more incidents.

Captain Griger recognized these inefficiencies and was looking for new strategies and solutions that could help connect their community. He knew from reviewing post-incident reports that many incidents could have been prevented if his community-wide teams had been aware of early warning signs. See Something, Say Something and Crime Stoppers were in place in the community, but they were not receiving the warning signs they needed. He was concerned that people were not coming forward because they did not want to get in trouble for being a snitch, they didn't want to get involved or get friends or others involved, or they simply did not trust the law enforcement reporting options available.

Forty-five miles away from Sarpy County, the Lincoln Public Schools system was successfully utilizing the First Preventers Program and platform. Captain Griger became aware of their successes thanks to collaboration efforts with the local Association of Threat Assessment Professionals (ATAP). With a bigger landscape than the Lincoln Public Schools district, Sarpy County had even more gaps, more silos, and more disconnects to deal with and was even more in need of the right community-wide approach to fix them.

In 2016, Captain Griger led the way in implementing the county-wide First Preventers Program for Sarpy County. He and the sheriff held a press conference that was attended by the county's five police chiefs and the four superintendents who represented the county's four school districts. At the press conference, they explained how every student, faculty and staff member, parent, and member of the general public could access any of the Sarpy County school websites, click an icon, and report red flags, concerning behaviors, and suspicious activities confidentially or anonymously and the information would automatically be routed to the right team members who could do the right things. In the first seventy days after the implementation and announcement of the community-wide program and web-based platform, one hundred new red flags and pieces of information were reported—far more than the law enforcement options had been receiving. This was due to the

> **The reporting and proactive community-wide intervention and prevention continues to this day because people saw proactive actions and results.**

approachability options of the new platform and the community-wide TAT strategy behind it. Sarpy County now had offense and defense working together on a more effective central information-sharing platform. The reporting and proactive community-wide intervention and prevention continues to this day because people saw proactive actions and results after their first preventer reports were submitted.

PREVENTION SUCCESS STORY: AMY'S CASE

One Friday night in Sarpy County, an incident report came in and was automatically and immediately routed to the appropriate community-wide TAT members for suicide-related issues. Tom,[26] a high school student, had gone to his school's website, clicked the icon, and filed an incident report on his girlfriend Amy's[27] suicide ideation.

When Tom clicked Submit, he had done his job as a first preventer. The First Preventer Platform securely shared this information with a community-wide team of people who had been predesignated to

---

26   Not his real name.

27   Not her real name.

be notified to respond to an incident of this type. In this case, the information was sent to the principal, a social worker, and the county sheriff's office, who were the members of the prevention team designated to be notified of a suicide threat.

Within thirty minutes, law enforcement and a social worker arrived at Amy's home, where she lived with her mother. The mother was unaware of her daughter's suicidal ideations and mental state. The social worker and a police officer sat down and spoke with Amy, Tom, and Amy's mother. In this way, the people closest to her learned about her struggle and were able to immediately help her. The next steps involved getting the school counselor involved so that Amy would have an ongoing support team of first preventers to turn to when she found herself struggling again.

Amy's suicide ideation story is an example of first preventers and first responders working together as a coordinated TAT to prevent a tragedy. As a first preventer, the boyfriend started a series of proactive actions that involved community-based first preventers and school-based first preventers who could intervene and provide Amy with much-needed support.

COMMUNITY TEAMS AND ROLES

Just as there are different roles for first responders (e.g., law enforcement, EMTs, firefighters), there are different roles for first preventers. Part II will look at how to build a team in more detail, but for now, suffice it to say that there are some key personnel who need to be involved in any team to ensure that there is always an effective community-wide team of heroes ready and trained to take action.

For example, in a case like Amy's, the officer, social worker, principal, and school counselor may be listed as team members who are to be notified immediately by the community-wide platform. Depending on strategies and policies in place, the sheriff's office, as a 24/7 organization, could call each of the team members to ensure they saw the notification and saw the incident report and ensure the appropriate team members are en route to the student's house. On an ongoing basis, each team member can add updates to the community-wide platform as they happen to ensure good information flow and awareness across the whole team. If the social worker and law enforcement go to her house late on a Friday night and do not contact anyone else that night, the school counselor and principal or others on the team would have a complete overview available to them on Monday morning so that they can get involved as part of the ongoing support team.

All the information reported via the First Preventers Platform is encrypted and securely shared with only the appropriate team members to ensure compliance with the Family Educational Rights and Privacy Act of 1974 (FERPA). This ensured Amy's privacy was protected, but it also ensured the appropriate team members were involved so that Amy would not fall through the cracks. Unfortunately, individuals fall through the cracks all too often when first responders and first preventers do not have a centralized platform for incident reporting, providing ongoing updates, and ongoing intervention and are instead forced to rely on emails and meetings and other manual efforts.

TAILORING A PREVENTION PLATFORM

First Preventers Programs can be adjusted for different industries and needs. For example, financial institutions are required to follow the Suspicious Activities Reporting System's (SARS) federal guidelines. The First Preventers Program can be tailored to work here too.

For example, a teller—as a first preventer—might notice somebody acting suspiciously, taking pictures, or casing the bank. A loan officer could receive a suspicious phone call from someone asking unusual questions. This teller or loan officer can go to the butterfly icon and report these suspicious activities so that the financial institution's multidisciplinary TAT can immediately investigate, assess, and connect the dots using these potential red flags.

Similarly, if a senior citizen has been coming in for years to make Social Security check deposits and small withdrawals but is suddenly withdrawing $20,000, the teller is often the first preventer to notice something suspicious. Seniors are often the target of people befriending them for nefarious purposes. A teller who notices suspicious activity in an elderly customer's transactions may not be able to confront the senior or their friend in the bank but could go online and report these suspicions so the TAT within the financial institution is immediately and automatically notified and can get involved according to predetermined procedures and processes.

Another way a teller fills the role of first preventer is noticing potential money laundering via the cashing of suspicious checks. Since 9/11, reporting suspicions of money laundering is required under multiple regulations.

First preventers are not limited to tellers and loan officers. Any financial institution employee or customer could report something suspicious that could be money laundering, a potential bank robbery, or senior abuse. A report of someone taking photos of a bank may follow a different path of notification than the report of an elderly person taking out an unusual amount of money. Therefore, a bank, a hospital, a school, or a sheriff's office can and will use the First Preventers Platform differently, but what is the same is the ultimate goal—identify, collect, share, assess, connect, intervene, disrupt, and prevent a crime before it is committed or a situation escalates.

LAST WORD

On the offense, the center hikes the ball to the quarterback, who then hands it off or throws it to a running back or a wide receiver. The offensive linemen also need to do their part to make sure the plays are successful. Multiple individuals must work together in multiple roles and positions to make the offense successful, just as there are multiple individuals who must work together to execute multiple roles on defense to make them successful. In addition to strategies and execution, the offense and defense need the right tools—imagine one team with helmets, mouthpieces, shoulder pads, thigh pads, and shoes playing against a team that is wearing bucket hats, beach shirts, shorts, and flip-flops.

The challenge for organizations and communities today is that there is so much information being observed by first preventers in their various roles and from various sources, but organization-wide and community-wide, teams are still using outdated tools and trying to manage this information with meetings, emails, voice mails, paper, spreadsheets, and silo systems of numerous types.

Communities will always need first responders because not every attack or crime can be prevented, but many more incidents can be prevented than currently are. For a total team approach to be effective, the TAT needs a comprehensive playbook so that first preventers understand their roles and first responders understand their roles and the whole team can carry the burden of prevention together.

With all the challenges, incidents, and tragedies facing organizations and communities today, depending on first responders only is not a wise approach. First preventers are critically needed, yet few organizations and communities have a First Preventers Program with the latest strategies and tools available to their first preventers to help them overcome barriers to intervention, disruption, and prevention. The next chapter examines these barriers in more detail.

SUPER BOWL SUPER GAME-CHANGING LESSONS FOR LEADERS

First valuable lesson	Game Changer
If you want to be a "winner," you need **both offense and defense.** There is an old saying that "defense wins championships," but has a team ever won a championship with the score 0 to 0? No! To win a championship, the offense must do its part too.	Organizations and communities need both offense and defense. Most organizations and communities focus on their defense, which is led by a defensive coordinator (e.g., security officer, police chief) and has defensive players (e.g., security, law enforcement, first responders, crisis response). How many organizations and communities actually have an offensive coordinator to lead their offensive players (first preventers)?
Second valuable lesson The Super Bowl has provided numerous examples of how a good offense can come back even after a horrible start and still win the game.	**Game Changer** Hundreds of organizations and communities have experienced and continue to experience horrible incidents and tragedies; it is time to regroup and equip the offense (i.e., the first preventers) with the right strategies and tools to start a comeback before things get even worse!

Third valuable lesson If existing strategies are not working, adjust them to achieve better results and have a chance at winning the game.	**Game Changer** Dissatisfaction with increasing violence, information breaches, lawsuits, tragedies, and numerous other incidents demands that offensive and defensive strategies be immediately adjusted and adapted so that offensive players (first preventers) and defensive players (first responders) can achieve better results.
Fourth valuable lesson Proactive and appropriate strategies and action are the real measure of intelligence and winning. When a team falls behind, the defense cannot be expected to also play offense.	**Game Changer** Proactive and appropriate strategies and action are the real measure of intelligence and winning. Action is needed to win the war against violence, terrorism, hackers, and other evildoers. The longer a community or organization waits to take the right actions, the farther behind it will be.
Fifth valuable lesson "It took a lot of great plays, and that's why you play to the end."—Tom Brady. How can these valuable lessons be applied to today's challenges?	**Game Changer** It takes a lot of effort and teamwork, with both the first preventers and first responders working together to win the game.

CHAPTER 5

BARRIERS TO INTERVENTION, DISRUPTION, AND PREVENTION

In almost every news report or post-incident report after a shooting, attack, or sex abuse scandal, facts show that multiple warning signs were reported in the days, weeks, months, and even years before the incident occurred. Afterward, when warning signs are made public, people cannot understand why nothing was done. The truth is, no one saw the bigger picture because the warning signs and pieces of the puzzle were scattered across so many people, places, and silos.

In 2017, a USA gymnastics national team doctor and former osteopathic physician at Michigan State University (MSU) was accused of molesting at least 250 young women and one young man under the guise of providing treatment. He was sentenced to 60 years in federal prison on child pornography charges. In 2018, he received two 40- to 125-year consecutive terms in a Michigan state prison after pleading guilty to ten counts of sexual assault.[28]

---

28   Eric Levinson, "Larry Nassar apologizes, gets 40 to 125 Years for Decades of Sexual Abuse," CNN, February 5, 2015, https://www.cnn.com/2018/02/05/us/larry-nassar-sentence-eaton/index.html.

The post-incident investigations showed that there had been warning signs for many years before his arrest and conviction. As far back as 1997, athletes had been telling multiple MSU officials that they were being assaulted. Many more young victims felt that they could not come forward at the time, and those who did found that their reports were covered up by people on the coaching staff or within the department.

Like many organizations, MSU offered an internal reporting option where individuals and victims could report a violation to someone within that siloed environment. The individuals who received the reports did not notify appropriate officials, and it later emerged that so much information was deleted from some incident reports that they were unreadable, and investigations were conducted in a silo behind closed doors. ESPN later reported there was "a pattern of widespread denial, inaction and information suppression of such allegations by officials ranging from campus police to the Spartan athletic department."[29]

In 2011, at Penn State University, a college football coach was arrested and charged with fifty-two counts of sexual abuse of young boys over a fifteen-year period from 1994 through 2009.[30] Again, no action was taken for years due to silos, cover-ups, and authorities

---

29   Paula Lavigne and Nicole Noren, "OTL: Michigan State secrets extend far beyond Larry Nassar case," ESPN, https://www.espn.com/espn/story/_/id/22214566/pattern-denial-inaction-information-suppression-michigan-state-goes-larry-nassar-case-espn.

30   Mark Viera, "Former Coach at Penn State Is Charged With Abuse," The New York Times, https://www.nytimes.com/2011/11/06/sports/ncaafootball/former-coach-at-penn-state-is-charged-with-abuse.html.

looking the other way instead of having a proactive team that contacted law enforcement.[31]

Sadly, stories like these continue to emerge. In 2019, Ohio State University released a report showing nearly two hundred students were sexually assaulted over a decade ago.

The University of Southern California is facing hundreds of lawsuits due to sexual abuse claims against a gynecologist that spanned a decade.

Cover-ups and silos are not just higher-education issues. A softball coach in Omaha was sentenced to ten years for sexually assaulting a minor. The principal of an Omaha Public Schools elementary school was arrested[32] for failing to report suspicious behavior by a teacher who was later charged for sexually assaulting six students in three schools.[33]

Analysis of hundreds of post-incident reports, going back to the University of Texas tower shooting in 1966, has revealed that there were usually more than enough red flags to prevent a tragedy, but common barriers resulted in failed prevention after failed prevention.

These cases highlight the common gaps and silos that exist when incident-reporting options do not feed into a central, secure, orga-

---

31   "Penn State Scandal Fast Facts," CNN Library, May 8, 2019, https://www.cnn.com/2013/10/28/us/penn-state-scandal-fast-facts/index.html.

32   Emily Nitcher, Joe Dejka, and Rick Ruggles, "OPS principal arrested, accused of failing to report teacher's suspected sexual abuse," Omaha World-Herald, February 8, 2019, https://www.omaha.com/news/education/primary-secondary/ops-principal-arrested-accused-of-failing-to-report-teacher-s/article_296d31c2-1cc8-5b59-81c6-2dd282484f56.html.

33   Alia Conley, "Former Fontenelle teacher appears in court on additional charges, could face 120 years in prison," Omaha World-Herald, December 22, 2018, https://www.omaha.com/news/courts/former-fontenelle-teacher-appears-in-court-on-additional-charges-could/article_e59a6ae4-7b68-5354-9a46-80904994b96c.html.

nization-wide, and community-wide platform that can collect and automatically notify the appropriate multidisciplinary team of first preventers. In hundreds of cases, information has gone to trusted individuals and/or into silo systems, where it was covered up or ignored altogether.

In addition to the lives that are ruined and the brands and reputations that are damaged, numerous other substantial costs are incurred by institutions who failed to prevent preventable incidents. For example, MSU paid a $500 million settlement. In 2018, the University of Southern California agreed to pay $215 million to settle a federal class action against the gynecologist.[34]

As situations like these occur and escalate over time, liabilities and consequences will increase unless an accountable and multidisciplinary team of first preventers exists to intervene and proactively prevent.

In this chapter, we will cover several common barriers that can have a negative impact on organization-wide and community-wide prevention efforts and successes.

AWARENESS GAP BARRIER

Lack of awareness is a huge barrier. Quite often, the leadership of organizations and communities is unaware that a new and proven prevention program exists to help prevent violence and improve the safety of children and adults in schools, organizations, houses of worship, and communities. Instead, they typically turn to their security leaders and even wonder if this could be the "new normal" for violence, shootings,

---

34   Nathan Solis, "USC Agrees to $215 Million Settlement in Sex-Abuse Scandal," Courthouse News Service, October 19, 2018, https://www.courthousenews.com/usc-agrees-to-215-million-settlement-in-sex-abuse-scandal/.

sexual abuse, suicides, terrorism, bullying, workplace violence, drugs, gangs, and numerous other acts of evil.

Awareness gap barriers and misinformation or rumors can leave people feeling hopeless, fearful, and even powerless to take action. Unfortunately, most people do not realize the role they can play or that they even have a role in preventing incidents and tragedies.

> Awareness gap barriers and misinformation or rumors can leave people feeling hopeless, fearful, and even powerless to take action.

Some people, especially children, may be unaware of what red flags and warning signs look like. For example, what constitutes concerning behaviors? What are suspicious activities? What are some of the different indicators of aggression? How does the average person recognize depression, suicidal ideation, or indirect calls for help? What should they do when there is a mental health issue? Many people are not aware of the mental health support and community resources that are available to individuals who are at risk to themselves and others. Law enforcement officers are not usually mental health experts or trained in the appropriate ways to engage outside resources.

Even when people recognized red flags and warning signs, there were other awareness gaps that led to failed prevention efforts. The Columbine massacre revealed that law enforcement knew that the kids were shooting targets, and the school counselor knew that one of those kids was struggling with depression. Parents had their concerns, and students had their concerns. Law enforcement simply did not know what the counselor knew, the counselor did not know what law enforcement knew, and so on. These are just a few examples of how awareness gaps make it extremely difficult for team members to take the right actions and prevent individuals and situations from escalating toward an incident or tragedy.

INCIDENT-REPORTING FAILURES

In almost all cases, post-incident reports revealed warning signs, concerning behaviors, and suspicious activities that were reported and documented but not immediately shared or were never shared with the right people. Frequently, an individual or a department might have thought it handled the situation but was not aware of the bigger picture—that is, it was not aware of incident reports in other departments, previous and related incident reports, incident reports from the community, or incident reports from numerous other sources (apps, text, hotline, web-based, paper, etc.). In some cases, the right people were not aware of information because of failed information sharing caused by cover-ups.

The MSU timeline shows the extent of the incident-reporting failure. It started in 1997 with one child's parents complaining to the gymnastics club and an assistant coach about the abuser's questionable medical treatment. They also talked to other gymnasts and found they, too, were experiencing inappropriate touching. In 1999, a runner made several similar reports to two coaches, which meant the abuser was also abusing the athletics team as well as the gymnasts. A softball player reported inappropriate behavior in 2000. A mother approached the abuser directly that same year.

Pieces of the Puzzle BEFORE
Lawsuits regarding MSU/Nassar Abuse.

From these warning signs and incident reports, it was clearly possible to take the assessment and investigation to the next level and to identify where other pieces of information were being siloed. The timeline legend shows pieces of the puzzle were with community members (CM), staff/employees (E), administrators/management (AM), internal security/campus police (SC), students/athletes (SS), friends/family of the abuser (FF), social media posts (SM), and law enforcement/police (LE). What if these warning signs and incident reports had been immediately collected and automatically shared with the right team members?

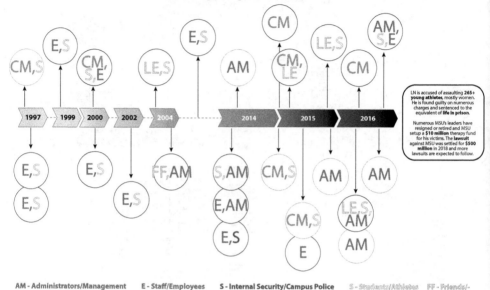

Silos of Information BEFORE Lawsuits regarding MSU/Nassar Abuse.

AM - Administrators/Management   E - Staff/Employees   S - Internal Security/Campus Police   S - Students/Athletes   FF - Friends/-Family of LN   CM - Community Members, Mental Health   SM - Social Media   LE - Law Enforcement (Police, Sheriff, FBI)

The post-incident analysis shows that children did as they were told—they told a trusted adult when something seemed wrong. In fact, they told multiple trusted adults. Unfortunately, even trusted adults (in this case the assistant coaches) may not know what other trusted adults know, and in some cases, they are trying to make their way up the ladder and do not want to be a snitch, especially if the accused (in this case the doctor) has seniority over them.

INFORMATION LEAKAGE

Information leakage can offer opportunities for proactive prevention. Information leakage can be a critical red flag that first preventers might observe and then share to generate actionable intelligence.

Information leakage can be accidental or intentional. Information leakage can be something overheard, something observed in person, something posted online, something someone else shares, or something else. Sometimes leakage can reveal a crime that took place or plans of an upcoming crime. Leakage can be a rant or blackmailing someone or part of a threat trying to scare others.

Here is an example of information leakage involving the Cal State San Marcos nursing student who killed one and injured three at the Chabad of Poway synagogue shooting near San Diego in April 2019. He leaked a four-thousand-word manifesto on the dark web, and before the shooting, he also set up a Facebook page where he planned to livestream the shooting. Facebook removed the page an hour before the shooting as a violation of its terms. There have been many other cases where information leakage was observed before incidents or attacks occurred; what if these information leaks could be collected and shared before incidents occurred?

Identifying leakage can be tricky if trying to use software to search for keywords on public-facing social media. For example, software might be programmed to flag leakage involving the word "bomb." A kid might post, "I'm going to go to the concert, and it's going to be the bomb," or a kid might post, "I'm going to go to a concert and I am bringing a bomb." Both posts might be flagged as leakage, but as false hits mount, people begin to ignore the alerts altogether due to lack of time and resources. People are a better way to identify leakage, as people are like walking, talking, surfing cameras, and people can tell the difference in the two posts above. The key is to make sure people have the ability to upload the leakage confidentially or anonymously and know that a team will receive their information and take action. Leakage is another reason why the butterfly icon was created to make it easy to collect the leakage quickly.

BARRIERS TO COLLECTING

The first stage of proactive prevention involves collecting information. Collecting information includes collecting red flags, warning signs, suspicious activities, concerning behaviors, current incident reports from multiple sources, previous incident reports, work performance, historical behaviors, previous interventions, investigations, and so on. Most organizations offer multiple incident-reporting options, which is good, except multiple ways to report information usually results in multiple silos, disconnects, and other barriers to collecting the information in a central way so TAT members can access it to see the bigger picture. This is especially true when the information collected spans weeks, months, or years and options and systems have changed multiple times.

TRUST BARRIERS

There are multiple reasons why trust barriers can exist. Let's start with common guidance for people to contact law enforcement using options such as See Something, Say Something or Crime Stoppers or direct calls. First, many people do not trust a law enforcement website or law enforcement hotline as being truly anonymous. Many believe law enforcement can track and identify people who contact them, and recent headlines and incidents involving federal law enforcement agencies have only made trust barriers worse. And there are other trust concerns because while it is good that Crime Stoppers offers rewards for tips, how do they know to whom to pay the reward if the tip was anonymous?

There are community engagement trust barriers—that is, when people call law enforcement, they often are forced to deal with long wait times on hold or a long response time, which creates trust and dependability barriers. Trust barriers like these can happen in large and small communities where there are limited resources to deal with increasing numbers of incidents. Community engagement trust barriers are a dangerous trend because the more people see no response, a slow response, or no action at all, the more likely they are to stop calling and stop reporting suspicious activities, red flags, or warning signs in the future.

TRUSTED ADULTS BARRIERS

Ironically, trusted adults can be a trust barrier during the collecting stage. Children are told from a very young age to report suspicious behaviors or concerns to a trusted adult. However, a trusted adult's response or lack of response can be clouded by biases or politics, and one trusted adult may view a situation completely differently than another trusted adult. In addition, one trusted adult does not necessarily know what other trusted adults know, which means most do not have a clear view of the bigger picture. So trusted adults can become accidental silos and barriers.

Another challenge is that a trusted adult, such as a teacher, may think he or she addressed an incident in their classroom but may not be aware of incidents taking place outside the classroom or online, so the child may lose trust in the trusted adult's ability to help. Here is a common example: One kid tells a teacher that another kid is bullying him. The teacher may talk to the bully and think they have handled the problem. Unfortunately, the teacher likely does not know what is happening in the next class or on the school bus or what is happening on social media or at home. Nevertheless, the teacher believes they solved the problem because they don't know the rest of the story. In some situations, the teacher talking to the bully could even make the situation worse if they do not know what else is happening. The bully could respond by saying to the kid, "I can't believe you told the teacher on me. Now you're really going to get it!"

Trusted adults may also lack authority; for example, teachers, counselors, nurses, bus drivers, and others may not have the authority to address certain issues. Other trusted adults may have limitations on the extent to which they feel comfortable getting involved.

> Sadly, trusted adults often end up creating trust barriers by becoming silos.

Sadly, trusted adults often end up creating trust barriers by becoming silos. Because each trusted adult may have different pieces of the puzzle involving individuals or situations, it is best to have all trusted adults report the information they have become aware of and collected to a central organization-wide or community-wide platform that collects all information so it can be securely shared with the appropriate TAT members.

ANONYMITY BARRIERS

Most incident-reporting options fail to offer a truly anonymous incident-reporting option. Asking an individual to provide an email means they will be identified. Phone calls are not anonymous because of caller ID. Text messaging is not anonymous because the number of the person texting is identified. Apps are not anonymous, because when apps are downloaded, the app's server establishes a connection with the user's phone—think about the customized preferences most apps offer. Another challenge with apps is that most were developed with ease of use as a primary requirement rather than security, privacy, and confidentiality, which can leave the data in apps open to other apps and open to privacy- and security-related breaches. Anonymity is a huge barrier for many people who need to be assured anonymous protections are real before they will make an incident report.

Some organizations believe they are solving anonymity by purchasing an anonymous texting solution, and they tell their employees, students, and others the text line is anonymous. However, most anonymous texting options just mean that when a text is sent, it is routed through a third-party service provider who passes along the reported information without revealing the identity or identifying number of the person who submitted the text. Students have been known to test the new anonymous texting option by sending a text on Friday evening saying they are going to commit suicide that weekend. The third-party service provider passes along the message that a student is going to commit suicide, but the receiving organization does not know who the student is because that information is not shared. In a situation like this, what can the organization do?

When this scenario is shared at conferences or seminars, most of the audience say that they would contact the third-party service provider and demand the identity of the person who texted they are considering suicide in order to help them. In that scenario, when authorities show up at the student's house and ask if they are suicidal, they find the student was not actually considering suicide; the student was only testing to see if the anonymous text option was truly anonymous. When the student realizes it is not, he or she usually tells others, and word travels fast that the anonymous texting is not really anonymous. The organization has just created a huge trust barrier, and many will stop using the texting option. Therefore, it is better to tell people that texting options are confidential rather than anonymous, which builds trust and ultimately helps organizations collect more red flags and warning signs.

USER-(UN)FRIENDLY BARRIERS

One of the best and easiest (and potentially anonymous) incident-reporting and collection options is a web-based option. When organizations implement a web-based option, most will have their webmaster place an icon or a link on their website that takes the person to an incident-reporting form. Unfortunately, these icons and links often end up buried on a secondary webpage that can be difficult to find, which creates a barrier for people trying to share red flags and warning signs.

Where are your incident-reporting options/icons? Are they buried several clicks or several layers deep on a department web page like security or safety or other pages? This can make the icon difficult to find, especially for people who are not technology savvy enough to navigate multiple clicks to get to the icon. Therefore, one of the barriers to incident reporting is simply finding the icon or link to make an incident report. The best way to eliminate this barrier is to make sure the incident-reporting icon is recognizable and easy to find on the home page of the organization's website.

Another common barrier with web-based forms (including paper-based or other forms) is they are set up as a generic form for all incident types and do not ask the right questions to gather the right information that would give your TATs a better understanding of the incident. For example, questions for a weapons-related incident should be different from a suicidal ideation incident and different again from a workplace violence incident.

Texting can be a good way to report information; however, text options do not include a list of questions to help guide people about what information and details are needed. People may want to report that they observed something suspicious, but they may not know what critical information is needed to help TAT members take the right actions. The result is that actionable information may not be included, which can leave TAT members confused, ill informed, and unable to act appropriately.

BARRIERS TO INVESTIGATION

TATs struggle with many common investigation barriers. Some TAT members are not trained on how to conduct investigations, roles may not be clearly defined, and guidelines for different incident types may not be clear. Other investigation barriers may involve how to deal with multiple case management systems, multiple documentation silos, multiple investigators and investigations over time, external investigation resources, privacy regulations, legal due diligence, and collecting information on an ongoing basis from multiple internal and external sources.

LACK OF DATA ACCESS

Data access for team members is a huge barrier. Access barriers due to multiple siloed incident-reporting options often result in team members not seeing all the data. Research repeatedly reveals how teams were not able to access historical incident reports, including red flags, investigations, or interventions that took place previously.

As a result, they cannot tell if a new incident report indicates the at-risk individual or situation is escalating. Related data may not be accessible for numerous reasons due to being scattered across departments, across multiple documentation media (e.g., paper, spreadsheets, emails, databases, case management systems), and across multiple trusted adults.

Without access to all the related data that has been reported and collected, team members are not able to perform valuable data analytics, including identifying trends and patterns with the individuals involved. Unfortunately, this creates dangerous barriers to the effective investigation of incident reports and at-risk individuals.

BARRIERS TO ASSESSING

Once an incident report has been received and automatically shared with the appropriate team members, and additional collection actions and efforts are completed, the next step for team members is assessing the information, the situation, and the at-risk individual involved. The assessment stage, which will be discussed in more detail in chapter 7, is a comprehensive and ongoing process of assessing at-risk individuals by using behavior, aggression, violence, mental health, stressors, and other types of assessments. The goal of the assessments is to establish a clearer understanding of the at-risk individual or individuals involved, as well as to determine what other resources may be needed to support the at-risk individual and what types of ongoing follow-ups and resources will be necessary. The assessments can also help establish a priority level, such as high, moderate, or low, so that actions can be prioritized and taken in a timely fashion by the appropriate team members.

Barriers to assessing are many, but some of the most common barriers include not having trained and qualified assessment resources on staff, not identifying assessment resources in the community before they are needed, not leveraging these resources effectively or in a timely manner, and not effectively utilizing assessment tools (e.g., behavior, suicidal, aggression, verbal/written assessment tools) due to team members not being trained on how to use, understand, and share this assessment information.

LACK OF AUTHORITY

Way too often we learn that TAT members did not have the authority they needed to contact, interview, or assess people in other departments or outside the organization. This often means the TAT cannot collect the additional information it needs. For example, a TAT member from HR, security, or IT may not have the authority to investigate other department managers. In other cases, they may not have authority to investigate an at-risk individual's family member or an at-risk individual who is an ex-employee, client, or patient. One or more TAT members need to have the authority and ability to investigate and assess, or they need to have direct access to other internal and external resources who have authority in order to continue investigating and following up with at-risk individuals and situations. When they do not, at-risk individuals can fall through the cracks, and bad things can happen.

LACK OF TEAM ORGANIZATION

Post-incident reports reveal recurring failures when TAT members are not aware of their specific roles and responsibilities during the process of proactive preventing. For example, even when organizations had TATs, it was not clear who was supposed to meet with the victim, who was supposed to meet with the perpetrator, or who was supposed to meet with other internal and external contacts.

Other common challenges, gaps, and disconnects arose due to roles not being defined based on a team member's expertise. For example, some team members are better qualified to perform interviews, some are better qualified to work with external resources (such as law enforcement), and some are better qualified than others to work with mental health assessments. The organization of a TAT is similar to team sports, where different people need to have different expertise that needs to be utilized in the best position to help the team achieve the best results. Team organization is a vital part of creating an effective First Preventers Program.

LACK OF TRAINING

Team members are often selected and assigned to the TAT, but sometimes they are not trained. A team member without appropriate training in conducting investigative interviews may come across as intrusive, accusatory, or biased. A lack of training can shut down interviewees and create missed opportunities to collect critical pieces of the puzzle. Lack of training on key components of privacy guidelines and policies, such as the Health Insurance Portability and Accountability Act of 1996 (HIPAA) and the Family Educational Rights and Privacy Act (FERPA) can create costly disconnects with information sharing and assessing. Post-incident reports expose how lack of training has led to important and sensitive information not being shared because TAT members did not understand how they could legally and securely share student records, sensitive records, and so on.

Another cause of prevention failures comes from lack of training in how to correctly document information from interviews, investigations, interventions, and other actions in a way that meets privacy criteria while still being accessible to other relevant TAT members (including community-wide TAT members and resources) who need to see updates and new pieces of the puzzle in an ongoing intervention effort.

Ultimately, lack of proper first preventer training for TAT members and other first preventers (management, board members, employees, students, resources, etc.) allows gaps, disconnects, and misunderstandings to continue to exist and prevention efforts to continue to fail.

COMMUNICATION AND COLLABORATION BARRIERS

Barriers exist when previous communications and collaboration efforts were not completed, documented, recorded, or shared. This makes conducting ongoing assessments and taking appropriate intervention actions difficult because critical pieces of the puzzle might be missing.

Communication barriers exist when team members are limited to in-person meetings, paper-sharing efforts, emails, voice mails, and other decentralized efforts. Figuring out how to get the entire TAT together for meetings is a perpetual challenge for many teams, especially community-wide TATs. If even one team member is missing from a meeting, critical information may not be shared, and an assessment or intervention can be stalled.

After Congresswoman Gabrielle Giffords was shot in 2011 in Arizona, it emerged that law enforcement had key information about the shooter and that the community college had other key pieces of information. Despite being called to the shooter's house multiple times for weapons complaints, law enforcement was not aware of threats the shooter made at the college or the videos he was posting online. These pieces of the puzzle could have been connected with more effective communications and collaboration strategies and tools.

Communication and collaboration barriers can be even greater when the team includes members of the community who are external to the school or organization. More effective and proven communications and collaboration is vital to ensure external team members such as law enforcement, social workers, third-party employee assistance programs (EAPs), information technology experts, and legal counsel are not limited to meetings and other ineffective options.

FEAR OF SNITCHING

There is an old staying that "snitches get stitches," meaning if you snitch, you might get beaten up, attacked, harassed, fired, or worse. The lack of trusted, truly anonymous, non–law enforcement, and easy-to-find-and-use incident-reporting options are common reasons why the fear of snitching keeps students, employees, family, friends, and community members from submitting incident reports and sharing the critically needed red flags and warning signs that TATs need.

Snitching is not just a barrier for kids. In the Sandy Hook shooting, it was discovered that the shooter's mother was scared to report red flags and behavior concerns about her son. The son had already cut off all communications with his mother except via email. She wasn't allowed in his room in the months before he shot twenty-six people, twenty of whom were children. His mom was leaking her concerns to some friends, but fearing her son, she did not go to law enforcement, other community resources, or the school itself. This is one of many examples where parents were aware of red flags but did not believe they had an anonymous or trusted way to report what they knew.

Snitching barriers are not limited to shooters. Human traffickers often check the phones of the children they are trafficking to see if they called helplines to snitch. Drug dealers threaten to do serious harm to the drug runners and their family members if they snitch. Kids and adults being bullied are warned not to snitch. Tip lines, especially law enforcement tip lines, are often perceived as snitch lines; however, the butterfly effect and the butterfly icon can be positioned as helping others, especially when the butterfly icon is placed on non–law enforcement websites.

EXPERTISE BARRIERS

Internal TATs often lack the expertise or resources in areas such as behavioral assessment, mental health, psychology, gangs, and terrorism. This creates potential barriers in the assessment stage. Behavioral assessment expertise is a highly specialized area, and in many cases, team members have to seek out behavioral assessment resources external to the organization. In some cases, these resources can be a great distance away. Teams need to have access to qualified expertise to handle different types of threat assessments, including behavioral assessments, mental health assessments, and suicide risk assessments. Knowing how and where to find experts and connect with them in a way that is secure and confidential can eliminate barriers that stop an assessment from moving forward and team members from taking action.

BARRIERS TO CONNECTING THE DOTS

Once an incident report has been received and the initial investigation and assessments have begun, team members need to work together to connect all the dots. For example, connecting all related data that has been collected, including historical incident reports, investigations, assessments, interventions, and other related information. Connecting the information with the appropriate support and potential intervention resources such as mentors, counselors, social workers, EAP, nonprofit organizations, community-based government agencies (probation, justice, attorneys, mental health), and law enforcement (local, county, state, and federal) for their review and feedback. Connecting the dots includes assigning roles and responsibilities to the appropriate team members, who will make sure the at-risk individual remains connected and supported and does not fall through the gaps.

LACK OF TOOLS

One of the most common barriers organizations and communities face is not having the right tools for connecting the dots.

Failing to connect the dots is almost always a result of adding silo solutions on top of existing silo solutions and conventional "we have always done it this way" attitudes. For example, over the past several years, more and more silo-based incident-reporting tools continue to be added to existing silo-based incident-reporting tools. This has resulted in red flags and incident reports that are not connected because they are scattered across incident-reporting silos at the organization level (e.g., web, text, hotline, paper, verbal, departmental), at the community level (e.g., local See Something, Say Something; Crime Stoppers; nonprofits; suicide hotlines; gang hotlines; drug hotlines), and across the state and federal levels (e.g., Safe2Tell, Safe2Say, SafeVoice, state hotlines, DHS, FBI).

Failing to connect the dots is also due to conventional silo systems that are in place, such as case management systems, HR systems, student record systems, security systems, counselor systems, risk-management systems, and other silo systems that are not designed to share information within organizations or across community-wide TATs. The lack of having the right tools—a central secure platform with tools to collect, share, and connect all the dots and scattered pieces of the puzzle—is why so many interventions, disruptions, and preventions fail.

CONNECTING THE DOTS AND THIRD PARTIES

Third-party external resources are critical to successful connecting-the-dots efforts. Unfortunately, well-documented barriers exist because third-party resources are not being connected to the information or integrated into the TAT. They don't have a signed memorandum of understanding (MOU) and have not received the training they need on TAT policies and procedures, privacy regulations, secure information-sharing procedures, standards, and tools.

Too many times these third-party issues and potential liabilities are not addressed in advance, creating barriers to the team's ability to connect the dots and take appropriate actions.

BARRIERS TO INTERVENTION AND MONITORING

Barriers to intervention and monitoring can allow at-risk individuals to escalate and execute their plans of attack.

Some of the barriers are due to not having the right team members involved with monitoring and updating the behaviors of at-risk individual(s) on an ongoing basis. For example, after the Pulse massacre in Orlando in 2016, it emerged that the FBI had been monitoring the shooter for two years, but he fell off the bureau's radar because he had not committed a crime in that time and because the FBI could not keep tracking him due to surveillance policies and other civil rights limitations. What if a social worker or other third-party resource on the community-wide TAT could have remained in contact with the at-risk individual?

The Fort Lauderdale Airport shooting is another example of barriers that led to a failure to monitor. In this case, the shooter walked into the FBI's Alaska office and said, "I'm hearing voices that are telling me to go shoot people." However, because it is not a crime to hear voices and because the bureau did not have additional information and red flags known to the shooter's friends and family, he fell off the bureau's radar. Unmonitored, the shooter escalated. He executed his plan by shipping his gun to Fort Lauderdale and then flying to Fort Lauderdale, where he shot and killed five people in 2017.

OTHER MONITORING FAILURES AND BARRIERS

At-risk individuals who may be struggling with suicidal ideations often fall through the cracks because there is no ongoing monitoring or no ongoing collecting of information to know if the individual is escalating or deescalating or if the interventions are helping. Statistics reveal suicides are increasing for multiple age groups and continue at a high rate for veterans, so there is clearly room for improvement. Eliminating monitoring barriers and disconnects between the at-risk individuals and the TAT members can have a significant impact on saving lives and futures and on avoiding the pain a suicide causes others.

Workplace violence is another increasing problem even though workplace violence training and policies provided by hundreds of consultants and resources have been taking place for many years. Post-incident reports reveal the increase in workplace violence incidents is most often due to monitoring barriers with ongoing intervention and prevention efforts involving individuals who were known to be at risk and a potential threat to others.

A workplace shooting at the Henry Pratt plant in Illinois in 2019 that left six dead and six injured is an example of failures to intervene and monitor. In this tragedy, the shooter was going to be terminated, which meant the employer was aware the at-risk individual had work-related and behavior-related issues. Employees were aware the shooter had a violent temper, his friends and family were aware of his aggression, and he was on law enforcement's radar, yet the organization failed to connect the dots, intervene, and prevent this tragedy in the workplace.

Barriers in ongoing monitoring efforts limit TATs' ability to collect new and updated information they can use and connect with previous information to more proactively intervene in potential escalations with at-risk individuals. Intervention and monitoring are especially important with upcoming terminations and other work-related disciplinary actions that can unfortunately trigger at-risk individuals to escalate to attacks and tragedies.

BARRIERS DUE TO LESSONS WASTED, NOT IMPLEMENTED

Lessons learned from incidents such as Columbine, over twenty years ago, still have not been implemented in most schools today. Lessons learned from nurse violence, workplace violence, terrorism, and other acts of violence that have been occurring for years still have not been implemented across organizations and communities. Not implementing lessons learned allows common and known barriers to remain in place, and the barriers continue to lead to more failed preventions and more incidents and tragedies.

One of the most common reasons lessons learned are not implemented is because most people—especially organization and community leaders—do not have time to research hundreds of post-incident reports, and they do not know about the lessons and failures exposed by these incidents. So they end up implementing the same status quo solutions the other organizations have implemented. This is one of the reasons *The First Preventers Playbook* was created—so organization and community leaders can learn about common problems and implement better solutions without having to experience their own incidents and tragedies.

DOCUMENTATION BARRIERS

Documentation failures and silos are common barriers for TAT members. When incident reports, interviews, investigations, assessments, interventions, and other actions by internal and community-wide team members are not accessible in a central secure database that is accessible to all approved TAT members, these barriers can make it difficult to effectively intervene and prevent. When documentation is not done, or if team members leave the organization and documentation goes with them, these barriers can put TAT members in really bad situations. To see the bigger picture and understand what might be taking place with at-risk individuals over weeks, months, and years, documentation-related barriers must be eliminated.

Failed documentation barriers have led to embarrassing and expensive consequences and, more importantly, a lot of pain for numerous victims and their families that they never would have had to endure if the documentation barriers had been eliminated.

DATA ANALYTICS BARRIERS

It is nearly impossible to identify concerning trends and troubling patterns if your TAT cannot access data to perform data analytics. Data analytics can help define the preventive and actionable intelligence and allow for the proactive actions TATs need to take for more effective intervention and prevention. Unfortunately, barriers with data silos, data access, data sharing, and data storage lead to even more barriers in attempting to utilize data analytics.

A lack of data analytics expertise on the team can be another big barrier. Without this expertise, knowing which trends, patterns, and anomalies to look for and how to use them to achieve better results can create significant gaps in organization-wide and community-wide prevention efforts.

AUTHORITY BARRIERS

Lack of TAT leadership is a common barrier. This happens when there is no clear team leader who facilitates the process, has authority to make decisions for the entire team during each stage of prevention, and is responsible for making sure immediate and ongoing actions are taken. Prevention failures repeatedly reveal that even when a TAT with strong team members existed, lack of leadership or the team leader's lack of authority to make decisions as situations and individuals were escalating led to barriers that turned into failures.

Useful information and ideas for improvements may exist, but if the leader does not have the authority to implement new strategies, new tools, and other changes, then barriers exist. A leader lacking in authority may also struggle with instructing and approving internal and external resources on actions that should be taken. For example, the internal physical security manager may not have the authority to instruct other internal department managers and team members on what actions they could or should take based on previous investigations, assessments, interventions, and documentation. Turf wars, egos, bias, unions, seniority, and other issues can create these lack-of-authority barriers.

ONGOING AWARENESS BARRIERS

Barriers also exist because new knowledge and updated awareness, such as alerts, viral threats, laws, guidelines, policies, procedures, lessons learned, and training, are not shared with the appropriate team members on an ongoing basis. Ongoing awareness and accountability barriers can be costly, too, if your organization is involved in compliance investigations, legal due diligence, and insurability reviews.

LAST WORD

Barriers exist largely because people do not know what they do not know. They do not realize that they have gaps, silos, and disconnects until a violent incident or tragedy occurs, which is a pattern that has been revealed in hundreds of post-incident analyses.

These barriers are not insurmountable. Effective ways an organization can overcome these barriers at each stage of proactive preventing will be examined in Part II of *The First Preventers Playbook*.

THE SIX STAGES OF PROACTIVE PREVENTION

Analysis of failed prevention efforts in hundreds of post-incident reports has shown that in almost every case, not only were there more than enough red flags, there were also distinct stages and stage failures leading up to the violent incident or tragedy. Research and analysis revealed six different stages where these intersected and overlapped, where gaps and disconnects existed, and how one stage needed to be effective to make proactive prevention steps taken during subsequent stages effective. For example, the best TAT on the planet could be in place to assess red flags and warning signs, but if there are gaps and disconnects when collecting this information and/or gaps and disconnects when getting information to the TAT, they may not have enough information to see the bigger picture or assess and take the right intervention actions.

The first stage in proactive prevention therefore is the collecting stage—collecting red flags, warning signs, and other leakage. The second stage involves getting information to the right TAT members, who are trained and qualified to assess information, individuals, and situations. This leads to a third stage, where the red flags, assessments, resources, and other information dots are properly connected so proactive actions can be taken. The fourth stage involves using the information and resources to proactively intervene and monitor at-risk individuals who may be escalating and deescalating or planning an incident. The fifth stage involves ongoing prevention actions and data analytics to identify patterns and trends that can improve overall intervention and prevention efforts. The sixth stage involves learning lessons from all stages, identifying what worked and what can be improved, and then creating and sharing ongoing awareness for all stages with all appropriate first preventers to implement.

Ongoing awareness is essential because threats are constantly changing. Organizations and communities have to be able to adjust to new and changing threats; for example, mass shooters' targets include schools, higher education, workplaces, high rises, public gatherings, and even people on the road in the case of mobile mass shooters. Knowing what risks and red flags to look for, knowing what the bad guys are doing, knowing how physical and cyber threats are changing, and knowing how each stage of proactive prevention must be updated to be more effective and more successful on an ongoing basis is critical.

This part of the book looks at each of the Six Stages of Proactive Prevention and identifies what to look for at each stage and how to take effective action.

CHAPTER 6

STAGE 1—COLLECT THE DOTS

Most have heard the saying "What you don't know can't hurt you." But what about "What you don't know CAN hurt you"? This holds true for organizations and communities as well as individuals.

Every year, thousands of incidents and tragedies in schools, higher-education institutions, healthcare facilities, government agencies, and other organizations prove that not knowing about red flags and warning signs makes it nearly impossible to successfully intervene, disrupt, and prevent violent incidents and tragedies before they occur. However, we know from research, lessons learned, and numerous federal agency reports that the red flags were almost always known by others but were not collected, shared, assessed, connected, and acted upon.

In a 2019 report, the US Secret Service studied forty-one shooting attacks in schools and reported that all attackers exhibited concerning behaviors, most elicited concern from others, and most communicated their intent to attack before the incident.

This statement, along with the previously mentioned DHS statement regarding red flags, validates in multiple ways that the first stage of collecting red flags, which includes warning signs, concerning behaviors, leakage, history, and so on, is important to prevention efforts.

Why else is collecting red flags becoming more and more important? There seems to be a new trend gaining momentum—perhaps a paradigm shift—in which attorneys of victims are filing and winning more and more lawsuits by claiming organizations and communities "ignored red flags." Defense attorneys are apparently paying attention to the FBI, DHS, and US Secret Service reports that state in most incidents there were more than enough red flags exhibited and observed before the incident or tragedy occurred, so if organizations did not identify and address the red flags, they must have ignored them. Attorneys, and even state attorneys general, have used the "ignored red flags" strategy to win their cases, including huge recent settlements against drug companies related to the opioid overdose epidemic.

For these reasons and others, centrally collecting the red flags and addressing them by taking proactive-prevention-focused actions is vital to preventing incidents and other costly consequences as well as preventing the soaring costs of lawsuits and potential settlements related to ignoring the red flags.

As noted earlier in this book, collecting and sharing red flags, warning signs, concerning behaviors, leakage, history, and other related information can be difficult due to many common gaps, silos, and disconnects that must also be identified and eliminated using prevention assessments and actions.

ASK THE RIGHT QUESTIONS

A first preventers prevention assessment can assist you, your organization, and your community with the collecting-and-sharing stage of proactive prevention. Keep in mind as you review the questions below that it is important to ensure the collected information becomes actionable, because when people do not trust that actions will be taken, they may stop sharing vital information and red flags.

- Are incident-reporting options and forms (web, text, app, paper, etc.) easy to access by anyone and anywhere?

- How are you making sure internal people know how and where to make incident reports?

- How are you making sure people in your community know how and where to make incident reports?

- How are you making sure people anywhere on the planet can easily make incident reports if they see red flags on social media or become aware of red flags in other ways?

- How is information collected from various and multiple incident-reporting sources?

- How is information collected from sources outside your normal incident-reporting options? For example, how do your team members become aware of information collected by law enforcement, social workers, EAPs, family, friends, and so on?

- How is new information from each incident-reporting option collected, shared, and connected with historical information from previous incident reports, other systems, other individuals, and previous actions?

- Who determines access rights to the information collected for each incident report option and for each incident report type (bullying, workplace violence, sex abuse, suicide, weapons, etc.)?

- How is information collected from a hotline, text line, app, website, or other source securely and then confidentially shared with one or more of the appropriate team members within your organization so they can start taking immediate action? How is collected information also shared with external resources?

- How is sensitive information, such as underage nudity, criminal information, or proprietary information collected and shared, since this information cannot/should not be emailed?

- How do team members know when newly collected information has been seen and acknowledged by other team members?

- Are one or more team members available twenty-four hours a day, seven days a week, to collect and act on time-sensitive incident reports? Do backup individuals exist to cover sick days, vacations, and so on?

- How do you guard against a team member with a bias toward the collected information or individual(s) involved or a team member or department who tries to cover up the collected information?

- How do you guard against a team member who decides the collected information sounds like a hoax (which may or may not be true) or a team member being too busy to review the collected information?

UNDERSTAND THE PATH OF COLLECTED INFORMATION

Other collection related questions that leaders need to address and understand include the different paths of the collected information. For example, if your organization is a school, what does the path of collected information look like when an incident report is made to a trusted individual? What if a student shares a red flag or concerning behavior with a teacher, a parent, a nurse, a counselor, a coach, a principal, an administrator, a board member, a volunteer, an SRO, a student, or someone else? What does the path of collected information look like for each, and where are the gaps, silos, and disconnects for each?

If your organization is not educational, what if an employee shares a red flag or concerning behavior with a trusted individual such as a supervisor, a manager, an ombudsman, a union leader, an EAP representative, a security guard, a colleague, a vendor, a contractor, or someone else? What does the path of collected information look like for each, and where are the gaps, silos, and disconnects for each?

A thorough review can help identify and eliminate common gaps where trusted individuals inadvertently become silos or dead ends for collected information. Research reveals how challenges can arise when a trusted individual receives information from another individual, takes proactive action, believes he or she has solved the immediate issue, and takes no other actions. However, it is vital for trusted individuals to make sure they follow proper incident-reporting options so this collected information and the actions they have taken can be combined with other collected information, which can help organization and community team members see a bigger picture or an escalation with an individual or situation.

Another path-of-collected-information gap involves third parties who receive red flags and concerning behaviors. Numerous post-incident reports reveal how red flags and concerning behaviors were reported to law enforcement and documented in their law enforcement system, but rarely was the information shared with an organization-wide or community-wide threat-assessment team. When red flags—such as noncriminal incidents—are reported and not shared with a community-wide team, the at-risk individuals can fall through the cracks rather than receive the support and/or intervention they need.

ELIMINATE SNITCHING GAPS

As mentioned previously, the fear of snitching can be a dangerous gap in collecting information when people believe incident reporting is snitching and do not report red flags and concerning behaviors. Some people do not want to be a tattletale, and others do not want to snitch because they are concerned that "snitches get stitches." For these reasons and others, it is important to share how reporting a red flag or concerning behavior, no matter how small it may seem, could be the piece of the puzzle that saves lives, futures, family, friends, loved ones, innocent children, and innocent adults from being attacked, assaulted, or abused by an at-risk individual.

Snitching is one of the reasons the butterfly effect approach became part of the First Preventers Program, and the results can be an absolute game changer. Most people are interested in helping and doing good things for others, so helping students, employees, and community members to see how they can help others by sharing red flags and concerning behaviors has proven to be very effective. The butterfly icon reminds people about the butterfly effect and how one incident report could be the missing link needed for a successful and life-changing prevention.

ELIMINATE TRUST GAPS

Another common threat to collecting information is the lack of trust and other trust-related gaps. If people do not trust who they are reporting to or if they do not trust that actions will be taken, then people will not go out of their way to share what they know.

Unfortunately, the trust gap between some community members and law enforcement (local, state, and federal) is growing wider every day, and some people will not contact law-enforcement-offered solutions such as See Something, Say Something; Crime Stoppers; state hotlines; or others. To address this serious gap, the First Preventers Program offers strategies and tools that create alternate collection points (schools, universities, hospitals, banks, nonprofits, etc.) so that people can do their part to help without having to call or access law enforcement websites.

The right technology can play a vital role in building trust too. For example, offering real anonymous incident-reporting options can help people to share information if they trust they can do it without being identified. There are many reasons people may not want to be identified, so to collect the information they may have, you need to offer real anonymity. If your organization or community only offers options such as a phone number, a text number, a downloadable app, a web form that requires identifiable information, or an email address, you may be missing out on collecting valuable information that others know—and that your TAT doesn't know.

Other trust-related gaps can include outdated policies and pro-cedures that require an individual to directly contact a supervisor, a manager, a security officer, or other trusted individual with the information they have. While the policy might have seemed like a good idea previously, these days individuals need additional options to meet their trust needs.

A good way to help eliminate trust gaps is to use surveys that allow students, employees, community members, and community resources to share ideas and feedback. Surveys should be conducted on an ongoing basis to give people multiple chances to participate and to help establish baselines with certain performance and satisfaction levels. Asking well-thought-out questions, analyzing the survey responses, identifying gaps and concerns, and then taking appropriate and noticeable actions can help build trust and help people become more confident about sharing red flags, leakage, and other information they observe in the future.

For example, for several years now, we have been working with a nonprofit called Stand for the Silent, founded by a father who speaks at schools across the nation about the dangers and consequences of bullying and how it led to his son committing suicide. We conduct an online student survey after each assembly to learn more about what students think about bullying, cyberbullying, suicidal ideation, cutting, drugs, weapons, incident reporting, trust, and so on.

What we have learned has been very helpful—and sad too. The results helped to reveal serious concerns, such as only 18 percent of situations improving after students reported bullying. Students also said they quit reporting when follow-up actions were not taken or the results were not improving after they reported incidents, which means future incidents, red flags, and concerning behaviors may not be collected. Why is this a dangerous gap? The 2018 US Secret Service report found that most of the attackers in forty-one school shootings they reviewed were bullied, and they had a grievance or wanted revenge—even more reason to collect information and take proactive actions at the right time before individuals and situations escalate.

In the student surveys, over 90 percent of students said they would report incidents, red flags, and other concerning behaviors if they had a real anonymous option. Unfortunately, most schools do not offer a real anonymous option. The surveys also revealed that nearly one out of every three students knew of someone who was a threat to their school. Most school leaders were shocked and unaware of who students were referring to and surprised that nearly 33 percent of students knew of information that school administrators did not know.

MAKE IT EASY TO REPORT INCIDENTS AND COLLECT INFORMATION

Extensive research and survey responses revealed another dangerous disconnect that is way too common: the incident-reporting button or icon is too difficult to find and use.

To collect more red flags and warning signs, the online button or icon for information reporting should be easily recognizable (like the butterfly effect icon), and it should be easy to find on the home page of an organization's website. Too many times, the web-based incident-reporting option was buried two or more layers deep on a security department webpage or safety webpage, and sometimes all that is listed is another hot link or an email address. If individuals who are not familiar with your organization's webpage (such as community members, social media users, family members, etc.) cannot easily find a trusted, recognizable, and anonymous or confidential way to make an incident report, you may have just missed out on the key indicator or the missing puzzle piece that your TAT members needed to know.

As more and more red flags and concerning behaviors are noticed by community members and social media users, it is essential to make sure anyone can access a trusted incident-reporting option and then find the icon to upload screenshots, videos, text messages, documents, and other information when they see it on social media and before it is potentially deleted.

> Ease of incident reporting must also include asking the right questions for each incident type.

Ease of incident reporting must also include asking the right questions for each incident type. For example, do your web-based forms and scripts for hotline operators ask specific questions that will provide answers your threat-assessment team members need to know? Lessons learned reveal how people may observe a red flag or concerning behavior but not always know what other information your threat-assessment team members need to know. It is important to review your questions, because if a person is making an anonymous incident report, you may not get an opportunity to ask more questions.

GO BEYOND INCIDENT REPORTING

A common response after incidents and tragedies is for organization leaders, community leaders, politicians (local, state, and federal), and others to add more incident-reporting options. But it is important to remember that nearly every school, higher-education institution, organization, military base, and community already has and has had multiple incident-reporting options before incidents and tragedies. These incident-reporting options ended up being silos of collected information, and prevention efforts failed.

In addition to being silos, most incident-reporting systems (web, hotlines, text lines, apps, trusted individuals, etc.) do not automatically and immediately route the collected information to the appropriate TAT members based on variables such as the location and the type of incident. To eliminate gaps, silos, and disconnects in the collecting-and-sharing stage, your prevention strategies and your prevention technology tools must be able to securely collect incident reports from all sources and then share each incident report with the appropriate TAT members in your organization and even in your community.

Asking the right questions and performing a prevention assessment will more accurately reveal why your organization and community leadership need a central, secure, private, organization-wide, and community-wide platform to collect incident reports and other information from potentially hundreds or thousands of individuals and sources that consistently end up in silos.

SHARE COLLECTED INFORMATION

No matter which incident-reporting website, app, hotline, or text line, and no matter which trusted individual, community member, law enforcement entity, or other source provides the red flags, warning signs, or concerning behaviors, if the collected information is not shared with the right people who can take the right actions, prevention efforts will likely fail.

How is your organization sharing information with internal team members and resources?

How is your organization sharing information with external team members, experts, and other external resources?

Are you sharing information securely? Are you sharing information in a way that meets privacy compliance requirements of FERPA and HIPAA? How are you making sure only the right team members have "need to know" access to the collected information?

The First Preventers Program uses research-based strategies and technologies to ensure all collected information is immediately and automatically routed to the right team members whether they are internal or external. One of the best ways to explain the strategies and technology is to use a well-known risk management and insurance strategy where silo insurance policies are typically covered by an umbrella policy. Organizations might have property, general liability, workers' compensation, errors and omissions, cyber, and other silo insurance policies covered by an umbrella policy. Now think about the First Preventers Program as an umbrella program and platform that covers all the other silo incident-reporting options and collects information from any silo so it can be shared with the right team members and then acted on.

The First Preventers Platform is uniquely designed as a central, secure, organization-wide, and community-wide information reporting and collecting solution where anyone can simply click on the butterfly icon to avoid getting lost in designated silos across organizations and communities.

The First Preventers Platform eliminates confusion and dangerous gaps, silos, and disconnects so collecting information and sharing information is much easier and much more effective than conventional approaches.

Small schools in rural communities, large schools in urban communities, community colleges, universities, financial organizations, healthcare organizations, government agencies, entire communities, and even entire counties are among the early adopters who are seeing impressive and successful prevention results.

FIRST PREVENTERS AND COLLECTING

Too many people have lost their lives or had their lives changed or ruined because of prevention failures. Preventing more incidents and tragedies starts with collecting the red flags, warning signs, and concerning behaviors and then sharing them and acting on them at the right time.

Most people want to help and want to do the right thing by reporting red flags and concerning behaviors to help others in need, to protect themselves, to protect family and friends, and to protect innocent people from threats and attacks.

The First Preventers Program is a proven way to help and empower people to be heroes and to transform the way organizations and communities collect information and share the information so the right people can assess the information to take appropriate actions.

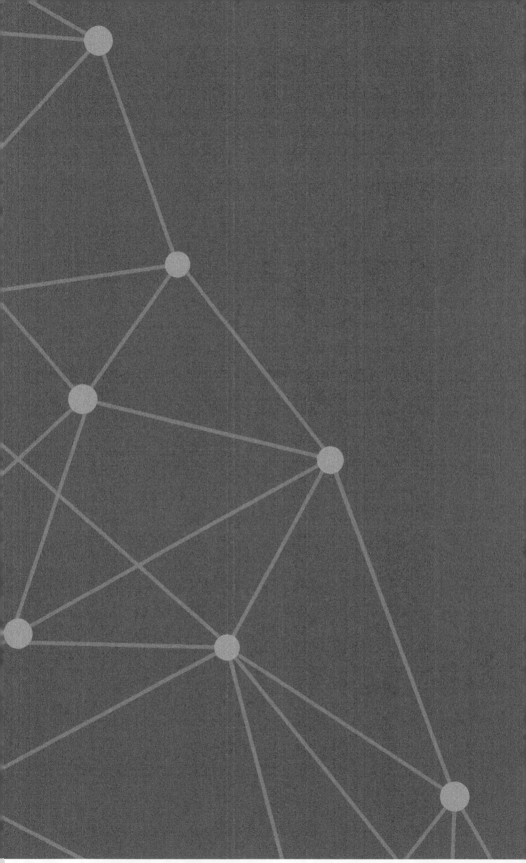

CHAPTER 7

STAGE 2—ASSESS THE DOTS

Assessing and threat-assessment teams (TATs) are not a new concept. In fact, most organizations have had TATs in place for many years. However, they may be operating with different names, such as behavioral assessment teams, behavioral intervention teams, behavioral assessment units, workplace violence teams, suicide intervention teams, safety teams, and others. In some educational institutions, campus assessment, resource, and education (CARE) teams exist to educate the campus community on bystander intervention, bias incidents, and crisis management, as well as monitor behavior and conduct threat assessments.

Because of several mass school shootings, such as Columbine, Virginia Tech, Parkland, and others, multiple states have passed or are considering new state laws that require TATs in schools. At the federal level, the Threat Assessment, Prevention, and Safety Act (TAPS) of 2019 was introduced to standardize a threat-and-behavioral-assessment process and offer training and resources for team members. There are also standards such as the American National Standards Institute (ANSI), OSHA, Joint Commission guidelines, and other industry-specific state laws that recommend TATs to address workplace violence, nurse violence, abuse, sexual harassment, and numerous other potential safety related incident types.

However, successful assessing is much more than creating TAT policies and assigning team members to the TAT. Each TAT needs to have the right combination of team members for each situation, and team members need to understand how to access and assess the information that has been collected in order to make the right decisions that will lead to more effective intervention, disruption, and prevention of different types of violence or other incidents.

All organization and community leaders must realize that most organizations—even at the federal level, such as Fort Hood, Navy Yard, Naval Air Station Pensacola, and Naval Station Pearl Harbor—had TAT policies and TATs in place, but they still failed to prevent acts of violence and tragedies, with Fort Hood experiencing two separate incidents due to failed prevention efforts. What failed?

ASSEMBLE THE RIGHT TEAM

In a successful First Preventers Program, TAT members are not just people named to a team. Team members should be selected based on their expertise and trained on an individual and team basis. They should be equipped with the right strategies and tools and given the authority to take the right actions at the right times.

Depending on the needs of the school, organization, or community, it may be necessary to create multiple TATs to focus on different incident types, such as workplace violence, community violence, gang violence, terrorism, weapons, sexual assault, or other threats such as suicide, fraud, ethics, and so on.

For each TAT, team members should include a combination of individuals with different skills and expertise from multiple departments such as human resources, security, legal, occupational safety and health, risk management, information technology, compliance, the board of directors, the union, the employee assistance program, counseling, crisis management, public relations, and others.

Creating a multidepartment and multidisciplinary TAT is critical in preventing cover-ups by departments and other silos. For example, multiple incidents and tragedies occurred and continued to occur for years at Michigan State, the University of Southern California, Penn State, and numerous other places where individuals from one department were responsible for assessing information involving an at-risk individual who was part of that department. If the red flags and warning signs had been collected and shared with a TAT that included team members from multiple departments, more than likely the right actions would have been taken much earlier. Additionally, a TAT with multiple departments, such as a legal department or the board, would have been able to save hundreds of students from being abused for years, as well as reducing damage to reputations, millions of dollars of costs to their bottom line, and numerous other costly consequences.

> In today's world, a community-wide TAT is vital to improving prevention successes.

In today's world, a community-wide TAT is vital to improving prevention successes. Community-wide TATs can include law enforcement, mental health workers, the county attorney, probation officers, juvenile justice, child services, social workers, and other government agencies. A community-wide TAT may also include resources from houses of worship and nonprofit organizations that focus on preventing suicides, domestic violence, drug abuse, gangs, and other problems.

ASK THE RIGHT QUESTIONS

A First Preventers Prevention Assessment can assist you, your organization, and your community with the assessing stage of proactive prevention. Whether you are assembling your TAT or looking to get the most out of your TAT, asking the right questions is key. You can start with questions that make sure TAT members know how to do the following:

- perform interviews of perpetrators, targets, witnesses, family members, etc.

- perform confidential investigations

- perform online investigations involving social media websites and mobile apps

- perform online investigations on internal networks, servers, and workstations

- securely share information using appropriate technologies

- prioritize incidents as low, moderate, or high to ensure appropriate actions

- ensure information privacy according to FERPA in the education industry

- ensure information privacy according to HIPAA and other state/federal requirements

- perform or assist in performing behavioral assessments

- document interviews, investigations, and assessments

- document assessment actions to meet audit-ready requirements

- document assessment actions to meet legal-ready requirements

- identify gaps, silos, and disconnects that could lead to assessing failures

- and more

TRAIN AND COLLABORATE

Knowing how to take appropriate actions in different situations requires TAT members to receive initial and ongoing training from specialists and experts in order to understand how to recognize and assess red flags, warning signs, indicators, suspicious activities, and other concerning behaviors. It is also important that each team member understand what actions to take based on the type of incident reported and the appropriate laws, industry regulations, safety guidelines, duty of care, and the organization's policies and procedures.

Guidelines can help with creating teams and team member training. For example, in 2018, the United States Secret Service and the National Threat Assessment Center (NTAC) released an operational guide for schools using a threat-assessment model and steps to follow in creating a comprehensive targeted violence prevention plan.

A United States Secret Service report from 2019 studied twenty-seven mass attacks in public places and provided information that can help TATs be more aware of previous lessons learned. For example, nearly half the shooters were motivated by a personal grievance related to the workplace, domestic issues, or other issues. Over half had histories of criminal charges, mental health symptoms, and/or substance use or abuse. All had at least one significant stressor within the last five years, and over half had indications of financial instability issues. Over three-quarters of the shooters leaked some part of their plan or their grievance prior to carrying out their attacks. With over 75 percent leaking their plan, imagine the possibilities if the leaks had been collected and shared with the right TAT members and proactive actions had been taken by the TAT and other first preventers.

Other guidelines exist for those seeking alternative or industry-specific guidelines for team-member training. For example, the American National Standards Institute (ANSI) along with ASIS International and the Society for Human Resource Management (SHRM) joined forces to release standards aimed at preventing violence in the workplace. The ASIS/SHRM WVP.1-2011 Workplace Violence Prevention and Intervention standard offers guidelines for policies and practices to more quickly identify threatening behavior and violence affecting the workplace, develop or enhance workplace violence prevention and intervention programs, and effectively manage post-incident issues. More guidelines are available from other resources, including OSHA's Incident [Accident] Investigations guide, the *Journal of Threat Assessment and Management* from the American Psychological Association (APA), and assorted resources for school administrators from the National Association of School Psychologists.

Once team members have received TAT training, more specific training should be provided on handling confidential, sensitive, and private information. Training on state laws and federal regulations, such as FERPA, HIPAA, red flags, open records, and the Freedom of Information Act (FOIA), is vital to ensure that accessibility and the secure sharing of information and data are understood by all team members. One of the most common awareness gaps involves FERPA and HIPAA, where organization and community team members are often not sure how to share information or if they can share information at all.

Sadly, way too many school leaders are unaware that under the FERPA legislation, sharing at-risk individual or student-related information with a law enforcement unit team as law enforcement unit records, though not student records, is allowed and protected. The law enforcement unit team can include the school's TAT members focused on safety and security. There is also a duty-of-care obligation, which can include the obligation to share information about an at-risk person with other team members who need to be involved so they can help. Similarly, HIPAA allows the sharing of information with appropriate people who may be able to intervene and provide services or support for an at-risk individual. However, many conventional information-sharing approaches, such as emails, voice mails, text messages, spreadsheets, and paper documents, are not recommended for sharing sensitive and personal identifiable information and can even lead to liabilities and privacy breach violations and fines. Issues such as these and others can be eliminated by using the First Preventers Program to ensure information is shared in a confidential and secure manner with only the appropriate team members.

Each TAT member should also be trained on how to work with outside experts, such as local law enforcement and local, state, and federal government agencies. Each TAT member should meet external resources before they are needed, and a memorandum of understanding (MOU) should already be in place with them to ensure policies, procedures, roles, responsibilities, and issues of information and collaboration are laid out before the team and external resources are knee deep in assessments and interventions. This emphasis on collaboration between organization-wide and community-wide TATs can make it easier to intervene and disrupt at-risk individuals who may be escalating toward committing acts of violence, radicalizing, suicidal ideations, and other incidents.

CHART THE CHANGING LANDSCAPE

All TATs need to establish multiple ways to keep up with new and changing threats.

Today's changing landscape highlights the importance of providing ongoing training for every TAT member because not knowing how to assess or what actions to take can result in tragic incidents with immediate, long-term, and other costly consequences. All TATs need to establish multiple ways to keep up with new and changing threats. Methods used to launch attacks are changing. For example, before 9/11, terrorist attacks involving flying commercial planes into buildings were not generally considered to be a real threat. Before a shooter opened fire on a crowd of concertgoers at the Route 91 Harvest music festival on the Las Vegas Strip in Nevada, killing 58 people and wounding 422, attacking an open area of people from an elevated location was not considered a real threat by most people. Before the attack in Midland-Odessa, Texas, a mobile mass shooter was not an attack most people were prepared for.

Unfortunately, terrorist attacks and mass killings are not the only tragic incidents faced by communities, organizations, and education institutions today. The #MeToo movement shows that TATs need to be aware of sexual-assault-related issues. They need to be aware of escalating gang violence, workplace violence, nurse violence, and suicides. Suicides accounted for more than forty-seven thousand deaths per year in 2017 and in 2018. Suicides have become the second-leading cause of death for youth between the ages of ten and twenty-four.

Another changing threat landscape is combining multiple attacks, such as physical attacks and cyber attacks, where terrorists (homeland and domestic) may use phishing, malware, and ransomware to block access to data, communications, or other vital digital assets and then attempt a physical attack too. As tensions escalate between nations, more and more experts are concerned about combination attacks directed at government agencies, utility companies, financial institutions, healthcare organizations, communications entities, and others.

To keep pace with today's changing landscape of threats, it makes sense for organizations and communities to create multiple TATs and even multiple community-wide TATs. The types of TATs and the team members for each TAT may vary based on the type of incidents, the type of organization, and the size of the community.

For example, workplace violence continues to be a major and mounting concern for most organizations. Workplace violence (WPV) TATs may be designated as one team or even multiple TATs to address different incident types such as employee violence, outside/visitor violence, nurse violence, patient violence, gang violence, parent violence, domestic violence, and others. WPV TAT members might include an internal or external resource from the EAP, mental health experts, information technology specialists, and local law enforcement. A member of executive management may also be included to ensure someone on the team has the authority to make decisions in different situations, such as terminations or discipline or ethics involving at-risk individuals. Finally, legal counsel can play a big role on the WPV team by ensuring actions taken meet legal requirements.

Weapons-related threats are a mounting challenge and concern for schools, organizations, and communities, which is leading many organizations and communities to create weapons-focused TATs, where team members are tasked and trained to identify, intervene, and prevent potential shooters.

In a school, a weapons TAT might include the principal and/or assistant principal, the safety and security director, the school resource officer or security officer, the counselor, a mental health practitioner, local law enforcement, and perhaps state/federal law enforcement. In an organization, the weapons TAT might include management, security, human resources, safety, the employee assistance program, risk or crisis experts, the union, a mental health practitioner, local law enforcement, and sometimes state or federal law enforcement. Other team members to consider for a weapons TAT may include a behavioral specialist who has expertise in identifying a pathway to violence and social workers who can provide support services to the at-risk individual and family on an ongoing basis.

Because suicides are the second-leading cause of death for youth ten to twenty-four years old, education institutions as well as other organizations may consider creating a suicide/self-harm TAT. The suicide-prevention TAT may include administration, such as school principals, assistant principals, student affairs, deans, counselors, safety directors, security directors, and other internal resources, as well as external members such as law enforcement, mental health workers, social workers, healthcare providers, and others from the community.

When Sarpy County implemented the First Preventers Platform, the sheriff's office and social workers were included as part of each school's suicide ideation prevention team. One of the reasons to have law enforcement on the TAT was to make sure the 24/7 law enforcement dispatch would be available to monitor incident report notifications submitted during off hours. An MOU was put in place to help make sure law enforcement was aware of roles, policies, and procedures related to FERPA so that they could take proactive actions and notify other TAT members based on the situation. Having a social worker available 24/7 has also allowed the school's suicide ideation prevention TAT to be proactive to at-risk individuals during off hours and more successfully assess and intervene with at-risk individuals.

A community-wide TAT with the right team members can help eliminate potential liabilities that administration and board members are concerned with during off hours and weekends. The good news is, the community-wide TAT has worked very well in multiple situations to intervene and prevent escalations of at-risk individuals at all hours when people are in need of help.

The First Preventers Program offers schools, organizations, and communities a research-based way to create the right strategies and implement a community-wide platform that all appropriate TAT members can access. This is the best way to make sure immediate and follow-up actions are established to support at-risk individuals on an ongoing basis to ensure they do not fall through the cracks, gaps, silos, and disconnects that are so common.

CLARIFY POLICIES, PROCEDURES, AND ROLES

Once the TATs and their team members are in place, policies, procedures, and roles should be reviewed (or created if they have not been already) and then securely shared with each TAT member. Because of state laws, federal laws, guidelines, standards, and legal due diligence, it is very important to not only share policies, procedures, roles, and training but also have documentation that each TAT member (internal and external) has reviewed and acknowledged their awareness and accountability for each document.

A prevention assessment can be extremely valuable at any time and for any of the Six Stages of Proactive Prevention, but especially when you are creating TATs for different incident types or making changes to incident reporting or adding new team members. Research and evidence clearly reveals that TATs will not be nearly as successful if there are gaps, silos, and disconnects in the incident-reporting options, red flag collection, and red flag sharing to ensure all appropriate team members have secure and immediate access to information as it is being collected from multiple sources. Remember, no matter how intelligent and well-trained TAT members are or how fantastic your policies and procedures are, if TATs cannot see all the information and the bigger picture involving at-risk individuals, it will be extremely difficult for the TAT members to make the right decisions and take the right actions.

Policies and procedures for TAT members should be clear on how to work with other team members as well as how to access, share, and protect different types of data such as:

- incident report data
- investigation data
- interview data
- assessment data
- previous assessment data
- historical data
- related data from internal departments
- related data from external resources
- intervention data
- analytics data
- survey data
- post-incident data
- and numerous other types of data

Policies, procedures, and roles help TAT members to be on the same page with how to collect, assess, connect, and intervene before at-risk individuals and situations escalate and a violent incident, act of evil, or other tragedy occurs.

COLLECT DATA FROM INTERNAL AND EXTERNAL SOURCES

Information sources can create major challenges for collecting and assessing data. For example, we previously discussed how multiple incident-reporting sources can create numerous challenges in collecting and sharing information. In the assessing stage, there are many other challenges that TAT members must be prepared to navigate to ensure assessing efforts are successful.

As TAT members are performing interviews and investigations, they must be prepared to collect even more information that can be shared and utilized by other appropriate TAT members. For example, trends reveal how more and more red flags and warning signs are being leaked outside the organization and observed by external sources than are leaked internally. Social media comments, behaviors outside of work or school, and other leakage can reveal vital information, so it is critical to have TAT members who have expertise in navigating social media websites and understand how to connect with others who may be directly or indirectly connected with at-risk individuals.

TAT members who are performing interviews and investigations will need to not only be creative and resourceful in reaching out to family, friends, colleagues, neighbors, and ex-relationships (ex-spouse, ex–significant other, ex-friends, etc.), but also be creative in offering ways for these connections to provide information in anonymous, confidential, and secure ways. Research reveals that numerous gaps, silos, and disconnects and the failure to collect information from these connections during interviews and on an ongoing basis resulted in

TAT members not having a clearer and bigger picture due to missing pieces of information.

Other external sources, such as behavior analysis experts, mental health experts, social workers, and others, must be part of TAT resources and available not only to be contacted but to provide immediate and ongoing information updates on at-risk individuals. As shared previously, timelines reveal at-risk individuals who have escalated and deescalated and re-escalated for weeks, months, and years. Assessing at-risk individuals over a long period of time and on an ongoing basis and continuing to collect information is necessary to help TAT members and other first preventers take appropriate assessment steps as well as other actions associated with other ongoing stages of preventing.

UTILIZE DATA ANALYTICS AND ASSESSMENT TOOLS

One of the ways to ensure a more successful First Preventers Program is making sure TAT members are trained in how to utilize data analytics and data analytic tools to assess and identify patterns, trends, and anomalies that may need special attention. For example, if an organization has received one hundred workplace violence incident reports (or bullying or other incident types), what do analytics reveal within the incident reports?

Understanding data analytics can help identify at-risk individuals and at-risk situations that may need additional attention. For example:

- How many incidents involve the same individual or individuals?

- Are any of the individuals involved exhibiting signs of escalating violence or aggression compared to previous incidents or behaviors?

- Are any individuals who were the target of bullying or workplace violence incident reports previously now the perpetrator of bullying or workplace violence toward others?

- How many total individuals are involved?

- How long have related incidents been taking place?

- How many individuals involved are internal to your organization?

- How many individuals involved are outside your organization?

- Are incidents taking place in the same department or same location?

- How many incidents are taking place outside your organization?

- How many incidents are spilling over into social media?

- What behaviors are common across one or more individuals involved?

- Are previous "false reports" now looking like smoke before the fire?

There are numerous other patterns and trends that could help TATs and community-wide TATs to identify at-risk individuals and situations that need proactive intervention and prevention actions.

Data analytics can also help provide or lead to more pieces of the puzzle that can help make assessments more effective and help TAT members achieve better results as they move forward with the next stages of preventing.

FIRST PREVENTERS AND ASSESSING

Any team, whether it be a SWAT team, a football team, or a surgical team, needs the right combination of expertise, the right policies and procedures, the right strategies, the right training, the right leadership, and the right tools to be successful. Would you schedule your life-or-death operation with a surgical team that did not have the right people, the right training, the right tools, and the right leadership to perform your operation?

TATs are no different when it comes to assessing collected information and then taking actions to get the right results, and their actions can be life changing.

The next chapter examines the next stage of prevention, which is connecting the dots.

CHAPTER 8

STAGE 3—CONNECT THE DOTS

Failing to connect the dots is one of the most common excuses heard after incidents and tragedies occur.

The 9/11 Commission Report found that the failure to "connect the dots" and failure to imagine what was being planned were important contributing factors to the September 11, 2001, attacks.

After the Parkland massacre in 2018, the FBI had to explain why two calls that came in via See Something, Say Something were not acted upon. One of the FBI intelligence officials commented that the FBI is continuing to look for ways they "can connect the dots faster while staying within the lines of what the laws provide."

Connecting the dots faster is important, but perhaps a better question is, If people can connect the dots within hours (or less) *after* an incident or tragedy, what can be done to help people connect the dots *before* the incident or tragedy?

As we have seen previously, the dots (red flags, warning signs, concerning behaviors, etc.) were observed and available *before* most incidents and tragedies occurred, but they were not connected.

While all the Six Stages of Proactive Prevention are important, the connecting-the-dots stage may be the most critical, and this chapter will further explain how the connecting-the-dots stage can be accomplished more effectively.

STRATEGIZE

How many times have you found out after an incident occurred in your organization that there was more information out there but your TAT was not aware of it?

Connecting the dots involves much more than just connecting the puzzle pieces that have been collected. Red flags and warning signs are not always in the form of a direct and obvious threat, so connecting the dots requires creative strategies to connect with other sources and resources who may have additional information. Sometimes one extra call by one of the TAT members can uncover the missing piece of the puzzle or the missing pieces of information that help explain the bigger picture.

When creating strategies, policies, procedures, and guidelines, organizational and community leaders must consider how connecting the dots needs to happen across their organization and across their community. For example:

- Who oversees the connecting-the-dots stage?

- Who has authority to contact and connect with other sources?

- Who has authority to contact and connect with organizational resources across department silos?

- Who has authority and responsibility to contact and update executive management and board members?

- Who has authority to contact and connect with community resources across local, state, and federal agencies?

- Who has responsibility to build and maintain connections and agreements with local, state, and federal agencies?

- Who has authority to inform sources on how to share sensitive and personal information?

- And other roles of authority and responsibility.

The leadership of each organization and community must understand the First Preventers Program, how it is implemented, and the actions that TAT members need to take to successfully eliminate the gaps, silos, and disconnects. This must be understood in order to successfully connect the dots and take the right actions to successfully intervene, disrupt, and prevent violence, tragedies, and other incidents.

LEARN FROM EXAMPLES AND TRENDS

In 2019, a shooter in Odessa, Texas, killed seven people and wounded twenty-two in a relatively new attack method for mass shooters—he was a mobile mass shooter who shot people in multiple locations across the community. Prior to the attack, neighbors called police about concerning behaviors, such as him shooting animals at night from a second-floor window. His closest neighbors called him El Loco, the crazy one, because his behaviors made them feel uneasy. A concerned ex-employer called police after the shooter was terminated from a previous job. The shooter then attempted to buy a gun but failed his background check. None of these dots were connected, but what if a red flag incident report had been submitted to a community-wide First Preventers Platform by law enforcement after they received calls even though no crime had been committed? What if the gun store knew about the community-wide First Preventers Platform and reported the individual after the failed background check? What if these dots could have been automatically routed to a community-wide TAT for a more thorough investigation? If just these dots had been connected, perhaps the outcome could have been different.

The Odessa tragedy and numerous other post-incident reports expose why numerous shootings were not prevented. When calls or incident reports are made to law enforcement—local, state, and federal—to report a red flag or concerning behavior that is not in itself considered a crime, the incident report is usually logged in the law enforcement database. It is not typically shared with a community-wide TAT because communities often lack a secure, central, community-wide platform where the dots can be connected.

When a First Preventers Program is implemented in a community or organization, red flags and noncriminal behaviors can be collected, assessed, and connected by a TAT or community-wide TAT. These efforts could lead to additional red flags that can be utilized to identify an at-risk individual who needs help or intervention before he or she escalates on a pathway to an attack on others and/or themselves.

To avert the distrust that comes when people do report red flags but see no action taken, as in a situation where a crime has not been committed, community leaders should take proactive steps to make sure they have a First Preventers Program, connecting the dots strategies, and a trained TAT/community-wide TAT in place so that actions can be taken even when there is no crime or no immediate threat. By taking action, widening trust gaps between the community and law enforcement can be reduced and eliminated and valuable first preventers' trust can be created when people know actions will be taken.

In 2017, a shooter killed twenty-six people and wounded twenty others at the First Baptist Church in Sutherland Springs, near San Antonio, Texas. It was the deadliest shooting in an American place of worship in modern history. The shooter was enlisted in the US Air

Force until he was discharged after being court-martialed on domestic violence charges. Before his court-martial, he had escaped from the Peak Behavioral Health Services facility, and afterward he was heard making death threats against the superior officers who had charged him with threatening a coworker. His court-martial meant he was prohibited from purchasing or possessing firearms and ammunition. However, it was later discovered that he was able to use air force base computers to order weapons and tactical gear for delivery to a PO box in San Antonio.

A great number of people within the air force and in his community, including his wife and the mental health facility, had pieces of the puzzle that were not centrally reported, collected, and connected. Additionally, the air force failed to record his conviction in the FBI National Crime Information Center database, which the National Instant Criminal Background Check System uses to flag prohibited weapons purchases. In cases like this, if there had been a community-wide option for people to report red flags centrally, and had the red flags been routed to a TAT, any one of the red flags from employees, superiors, family, or other community members could have started the process of interviewing and investigating his background with previous employers, the air force, family, and other people, which could have helped to connect the dots and led to intervention actions.

Research has exposed a troubling trend for TATs/community-wide TATs and connecting the dots, as more than half the red flags and warning signs that TAT members needed were scattered across sources outside their organization. Outside sources include social media, family, friends, neighbors, community members, law enforcement,

> TATs must be equipped to connect the dots with internal and external sources.

mental health workers, social workers, EAPs, nonprofits, houses of worship, and others. TATs/community-wide TATs must be equipped to connect the dots with internal and external sources; otherwise, TATs/community-wide TATs may see less than half the potential information available.

Family and friends are two of the most valuable external sources of information TAT members need to proactively connect with. To make sure effective communication with family and friends involving at-risk individuals can occur, it is important that organizational leadership establish the strategies, policies, procedures, roles, and guidelines by which this coordinated connecting-the-dots effort can happen. When organization and community leaders establish a safe, community-accessible non–law enforcement option, they can empower family and friends who may be reluctant to share information in person because they do not want the at-risk individual to know they are snitching.

Other often-overlooked sources of information that can help TATs connect the dots include ex-spouses or partners, ex-employees, ex-friends, estranged family members, and neighbors. For example, in the terrorist attack in San Bernardino, it emerged that neighbors of the terrorist attackers noticed numerous red flags, warning signs, or suspicious activities, but they did not feel they had a safe, trusted, or anonymous way to come forward with information they observed.

During the connecting-the-dots stage, leadership and TAT members should always consider any external sources that may have historical information or information about behavior changes that could help to connect the dots and lead to action.

ADOPT A CENTRAL CONNECTING-THE-DOTS STRATEGY

The more information dots available, the better the TAT understand situations and individuals.

A central comprehensive connecting-the-dots strategy should include several different sources and resources.

INCIDENT-REPORTING SYSTEM SOURCES

- Intranet website options/forms
- External facing website options/forms
- Organization hotlines (safety, security, ethics, whistle-blower, etc.)
- Text hotlines
- Apps (organization-based, community-based, state-based, national-based, etc.)
- Social media options (Facebook, Nextdoor, Ring, chat rooms, etc.)
- Community hotlines (Crime Stoppers, law enforcement, nonprofit organizations specializing in gangs, drugs, domestic violence, human trafficking, suicide, etc.)
- State agency hotlines
- National hotlines (See Something, Say Something; child abuse; suicide; human trafficking; etc.)

Information can be reported to hundreds of incident-reporting options, so having a comprehensive strategy and central platform to act as a funnel for connecting the dots is vital.

OTHER SOURCES: INTERNAL TRUSTED ADULTS, SUCH AS

- Threat-assessment team members
- Human resources department members
- Security professionals
- Safety personnel
- Counselors
- Employee assistance personnel
- Legal experts
- Risk experts
- Ethics experts
- Information technology experts

OTHER EXTERNAL SOURCES, SUCH AS

- Family members
- Ex-family, ex-significant others, etc.
- Friends (local, hometown, etc.)
- Colleagues (vendors, contractors, service providers, etc.)
- Social media (apps, groups, etc.)
- Neighbors
- Mental health (social workers, local government agencies, etc.)
- Law enforcement (police, sheriff, etc.)
- Judicial/county attorney
- Educational
- Public records

- Nonprofit organizations
- Faith-based organizations

Research and post-incident reports reveal most organizations and communities are attempting to connect the dots using old-school and conventional approaches that are typically manual sharing efforts, in-person meetings, paper shuffling, emails, voice mails, spreadsheets, silo case management systems, and so forth. As mentioned previously, most of these conventional approaches create privacy nightmares and other liabilities that could be prevented with more comprehensive strategies and more efficient technologies.

The following is an example of what a central comprehensive and community-wide connecting-the-dots strategy using the First Preventers Program and the butterfly effect icon might look like: when anyone in the organization, in the community, on social media, or anywhere observes a red flag or warning sign—or when a person receives a notification from one of the many incident-reporting systems—they can click on the butterfly icon and report their observations of a red flag confidentially or anonymously. The incident report is automatically collected and documented in the central platform, and the appropriate TAT or community-wide TAT members are automatically and immediately notified. In this case, the potential at-risk individual identified is John Doe, and he is an employee. The TAT members include people from HR, legal, security, IT, and ethics, and once the incident report is submitted all team members are notified. Once notified, the HR team member can immediately look up John Doe, and the HR team member may find additional information in the HR system where employee information has been collected over the years. The legal department team member may be aware of a previous incident, lawsuit, or settlement concerning John Doe. The security department team member can look up John Doe to see if previous security reports or responses involving John Doe have been recorded. The IT team member may be able to look into John Doe's company emails to see if his communications are related and/or concerning. Each TAT member can immediately begin collecting and connecting the dots and securely adding/uploading the related information to the First Preventers Platform to help the TAT connect the dots and produce a clearer picture for the team members. Connecting the information might reveal that John Doe has been exhibiting and sharing grievances, ideations, or threats and may even be escalating. As the bigger picture comes together, TAT members can conduct additional interviews with other sources and resources (e.g., family, colleagues, friends, or neighbors) who may have additional information and pieces of the puzzle that can be collected, assessed, and connected. Now with more pieces of the puzzle connected, TAT members can explore what the bigger picture is revealing.

> Collecting and connecting the dots can help determine the next steps.

Collecting and connecting the dots can help determine the next steps. If John Doe is exhibiting new or recurring behavioral changes—for example, his supervisor may notice that he is always late, agitated, or sleeping at work—these behavioral changes could indicate something has changed within John Doe's life. Connecting the dots may indicate a more in-depth behavior assessment and more investigation are warranted so the right intervention actions can be taken.

In a school example, a teacher might observe that a student has started sleeping in class, dressing differently, or showing up late or suddenly has falling grades. A counselor, nurse, or coach may also observe behavior changes. These behavior changes are not necessarily red flags or indicators that the student is going to do something bad, and they are not red flags that would normally be reported to a hotline (school or state or federal). However, many post-incident reports have noted that "a year ago, that student started changing." Connecting the dots sooner is safer and better for everyone than trying to connect the dots after an escalation has turned into an incident or tragedy, which is why TATs need to use imagination when a red flag is received to see if other behaviors could be indicators of an at-risk individual needing assistance.

These examples expose some of the biggest challenges in connecting the dots if organizations, schools, and communities do not have a central, secure platform to eliminate the gaps, silos, and disconnects and comprehensive strategies to bring all the pieces of the puzzle together so the TAT members can see them.

ANTICIPATE PRIVACY-RELATED CHALLENGES

As mentioned multiple times in this book, privacy misunderstandings can pose challenges for TAT and community-wide TAT members trying to collect and especially connect the dots if leadership and team members believe FERPA or HIPAA prevents them from sharing student records, employee records, counselor records, and other records with other TAT members or law enforcement. Therefore, leadership and TATs/community-wide TATs must understand FERPA and HIPAA regulations and be able to explain them to other team members, sources, and resources working on or with the TAT/community-wide TAT. In this way, everyone is aware of what information can be collected, shared, and connected and how, if the individual might be at risk as a threat.

For additional compliance resources, please visit https://www.firstpreventers.org/compliance/.

Remember, HIPAA and FERPA were not created to prevent information sharing if someone is a risk or threat to themselves or others; however, having the right strategies and the right technologies to connect the dots safely, confidentially, and securely is key.

FIRST PREVENTERS AND CONNECTING THE DOTS

Failing to connect the dots has been an excuse for far too long. Failing to connect the dots has resulted in way too many lives and futures being lost and ruined. Failing to connect the dots has resulted in way too many millions of dollars in losses and recovery. Failing to connect the dots has resulted in way too many first responders having to put their lives on the line and then having to deal with PTSD long term.

Connecting the dots is not that difficult when the right strategies and tools are in place, but connecting the dots is still not prevention. The next stage involves the actions that must be taken to intervene and disrupt at-risk individuals from escalating and executing their ideations, revenge, plans, and attacks on themselves and others.

CHAPTER 9

STAGE 4—INTERVENE AND MONITOR

Intervention refers to actions taken to intentionally become involved to help at-risk individuals and/or prevent the at-risk situation from escalating to something much worse.

Effective intervention must include ongoing monitoring of at-risk individuals and at-risk situations to understand what is happening currently and on an ongoing basis. Intervention, therefore, relies heavily on previous stages of effectively collecting, sharing, assessing, and connecting the dots so that appropriate intervention actions can be taken. If all the red flags have been collected and the dots connected, it is much easier to intervene and prevent escalations that could potentially become incidents and tragedies.

Once information has been collected and assessed, and the information and resource dots are connected, intervention is needed to disrupt at-risk individuals who may be escalating from a grievance to ideation, from ideation to planning, from planning to preparing, or from preparing to executing the plan, which could be anything from workplace violence to self-harm, an act of terrorism, or another incident.

The process of knowing who should intervene, how to intervene, and when to intervene may initially seem overwhelming. The good news is that multiple threat-assessment and intervention guidelines exist to help establish the processes that a multidisciplinary TAT should follow to get better results. Intervention models from the American Psychological Association can be utilized and models can be found for individuals, families, support groups, education, and others. Other guidelines like the Workplace Violence Prevention and Intervention (ASIS/SHRM) from the American National Standard Institute and the FBI's National Center for the Analysis of Violent Crime (NCAVC) guidelines and numerous others from intervention experts can help too. There are also intervention guidelines on specific topics such as school violence, gun violence, gang violence, domestic violence, drug-related violence, terrorism, and sex abuse.

Intervention guidelines can offer a good starting point. However, much like having a recipe for a favorite dish, just having the intervention recipe is not enough. Simply put, if just having a recipe were enough, violent incidents and tragedies would be decreasing. Clearly, something is missing and solutions are needed.

One of the most common reasons why intervention and monitoring fail is because the at-risk individual fell through the cracks created by gaps, silos, and disconnects between TATs, organizational resources, community resources, expert resources, and so on. Data analytics, improperly conducted or not conducted at all, can also contribute to intervention failures when TATs do not have all the information they need to intervene.

Monitoring, documenting, sharing, and analyzing ongoing behavior is essential at the intervention stage. Without these steps, TATs cannot learn or be sure which interventions work and which fail.

Missing information can lead to a misguided intervention that could actually trigger the person to go to the next level of their escalation.

RETHINK AND EXPAND RESOURCES

One of the common excuses heard after incidents and tragedies occur is that there was lack of resources, especially mental health and social workers, for ongoing intervention and monitoring. Often, upon further review, the cause of a failed intervention was related to a failure to leverage the resources that were available to TATs on a community-wide or statewide or nationwide basis.

For example, does your TAT or community-wide TAT have MOUs and policies in place to leverage your internal departments like HR, security, safety, legal, risk, compliance, operations, etc.? Has your TAT or community-wide TAT put MOUs and policies in place to leverage community resources like law enforcement, city/county attorney, city/county schools, nonprofit organizations, mental health, healthcare, faith-based organizations, etc.?

Has your TAT or community-wide TAT put MOUs and policies in place to leverage third-party experts and third-party service providers like behavioral experts, interview experts, employee assistance programs (EAPs), social workers, psychologists, psychiatrists, risk experts, insurance experts, social media experts, etc.?

Has your TAT or community-wide TAT accessed and customized intervention guidelines (government, education, nonprofit, etc.) for terrorism, workplace violence, school violence, domestic violence, gang violence, drug violence, sexual assaults, human trafficking, suicide, bullying, etc.?

Has your TAT or community-wide TAT implemented secure communications technologies to connect the dots and leverage your resources? Research indicates most TATs and community-wide TATs rely on weekly, biweekly, or monthly meetings, which are not timely and therefore not efficient enough to deal with today's fast-moving threats. In many cases, meetings are infrequent because most TAT/ community-wide TAT members have full-time jobs in addition to their team roles. When community-wide resources are added to the team along with FBI or local government agencies, getting everyone together for meetings becomes even more challenging.

Real-time resource leveraging is becoming even more critical to effective intervention because social media can escalate at-risk individuals faster than in the past. At-risk individuals can also escalate quickly due to changes within their organization—for example, a disciplinary meeting, getting fired, or being laid off. Similarly, being served papers, getting divorced, or dealing with financial stressors can cause escalation. These sudden changes can happen at any time, which makes leveraging resources real-time so important. The information presented at a monthly meeting could be days, weeks, or even a month old and too late for an effective intervention.

> Sudden changes can happen at any time, which makes leveraging resources real-time so important.

To leverage the maximum amount of resources available, it is also a good idea for the TAT or community-wide TAT to build relationships with colleagues, coworkers, friends, family, or others who might be associated with the at-risk individual. This will afford the team the option to reach out and ask these resources to update them on anything strange or different about the at-risk individual. To make it easy for resources to share observations and updates, these colleagues, coworkers, friends, and family members should be directed to use the confidential or anonymous butterfly effect icon, which will make sure additional information is collected in the centralized platform and the appropriate team members and resources are notified immediately to allow further action to be taken more quickly.

ESTABLISH INTERVENTION AUTHORITY

When intervention and monitoring expertise includes internal and external resources, it is important that authority is designated to avoid turf wars. For example, TAT members should report to the designated executive management person or one or more board members to make sure that two or more individuals (dual control) are responsible for overseeing and leading the intervention and monitoring actions. The 9/11 Commission Report asked the following questions: Who is the quarterback? Who is calling the play that assigns roles to help them execute as a team?

It is also important to establish and designate authority for community-based TAT members. For example, are there situations where a psychiatrist, law enforcement officer, social worker, or other professional should call the play for the team? It is important to review situations involving third-party resources and community-based resources to ensure there is no disconnect in authority to avoid a failure of cooperation that may cause an at-risk individual to fall through the cracks.

LEVERAGE EXPERTS

One of the best and most-proven ways to improve the intervention and monitoring stage is by leveraging intervention expertise and/or monitoring expertise.

For example, sometimes it is easier for external intervention and ongoing monitoring resources to stay connected with an at-risk individual when the at-risk individual is no longer part of the organization or no longer living in the community. Leveraging external experts (e.g., mental health specialists, behavioral specialists, psychologists, psychiatrists, social workers, legal professionals, EAPs, or local, state, and federal government experts) can empower TATs or community-wide TATs to monitor at-risk individuals that perhaps the FBI or law enforcement can no longer monitor due to surveillance limitations. No matter the situation, it is imperative that external experts are identified, connected, and coordinated to follow guidelines, which also includes understanding how to securely share ongoing observations and behavioral changes they observe. All appropriate team members need to see the updated bigger picture to effectively deliver and adjust interventions on an ongoing basis.

LEVERAGE DATA ANALYTICS

Lessons learned from post-incident reports show how data analytics can help experts improve intervention efforts and results. Data may include behavioral assessments, previous and current intervention actions, public records, law enforcement records, personal stressors, mental health issues, weapons, drugs, aggression reports, and data from other sources. Collected data can be analyzed to expose patterns and trends that may not be otherwise obvious and then shared with TAT or community-wide TAT members and intervention experts to help identify escalations or de-escalations and other potential changes that may require intervention adjustments.

It is important to monitor an at-risk individual based on their at-risk situation, which could be drug related, violence related, depression related, suicide related, weapons related, or a combination of two or more. In this way, data analytics can be used to help the TAT or community-wide TAT remain abreast of behavior history and recent behaviors so the right intervention and right monitoring actions can be taken.

CHALLENGE BIASES

Intervention and monitoring challenges can arise if one or more of the threat-assessment and intervention team members are biased. For example, a biased team member could decide an individual is or is not a risk or threat because of their political, racial, gender, religious, or sexual orientation bias. Bias must be addressed by leadership and by team members to eliminate blind spots in the intervention stage. For example, an at-risk individual may be triggered or may escalate if they become aware of bias toward them. Conversely, bias by a team member may allow an at-risk individual to escalate with little or no intervention or monitoring.

Intervention and monitoring can also be improved by rethinking strategies and biases associated with zero tolerance, suspensions, expulsions, and other disciplinary actions. Lessons learned from mass shootings in schools, higher education, government, and other organizations show it is very difficult for TATs to continue their intervention and monitoring efforts for at-risk individuals who were suspended, expelled, or terminated. Depending on the at-risk individual's pathway and escalation, being suspended, expelled, or terminated could be a trigger or provide the at-risk individual with the extra time they need to plan and execute an attack.

Therefore, creativity is necessary with some at-risk individuals. For example, an in-school suspension might be preferable to expulsion, or referring an employee to the EAP may be preferable to termination. This can give an intervention team and experts more time to review the at-risk individual's red flags, warning signs, behavioral assessments, and escalations as well as make sure other resources have all been contacted to better understand the situation. Ongoing monitoring and intervention are important in these situations to make sure the TAT can stay connected, making sure at-risk individuals do not fall through the cracks and making sure at-risk individuals receive the intervention and monitoring they require.

DOCUMENT THOROUGHLY

Proper documentation of intervention and monitoring actions is critical. Improperly handled documentation can lead to legal, compliance, risk, insurability, and other disconnects, liabilities, and costly consequences.

For example, lawsuits and liabilities are a mounting concern, and because plaintiffs' attorneys are becoming more sophisticated about standards and regulations, it is important that a TAT maintain compliance and keep thorough, secure, and confidential records of all intervention and monitoring actions and explanations for their actions. Why? Because attorneys are using a new strategy to sue organizations for "ignoring red flags," and they are winning because when organizations fail to prevent incidents or tragedies and red flags were available, they need to be able to prove they were aware and they were taking actions based on the red flags that existed.

Because more and more intervention efforts involve community-wide teams and external experts, documentation needs to take place in a central, secure, community-wide platform that supports external accessibility. A central platform strategy can provide significant advantages over paper-based, spreadsheet-based, and department-based systems; employee systems; student systems; and numerous other application-based and case management systems.

FIRST PREVENTERS AND INTERVENING

Intervention is the best way to prevent at-risk individuals from escalating toward an unwanted incident or tragedy. Successful intervention is a matter of being creative and thinking differently to achieve different and better results. Organizations, schools, higher education institutions, hospitals, and government offices will never have all the internal expertise they need, which is why the First Preventers Program and leveraging internal and external resources on demand

> Successful intervention is a matter of being creative and thinking differently to achieve different and better results.

in an effective and tech-centric way is the way of the future.

The next stage is the preventing stage, and it will be examined in more detail in the next chapter.

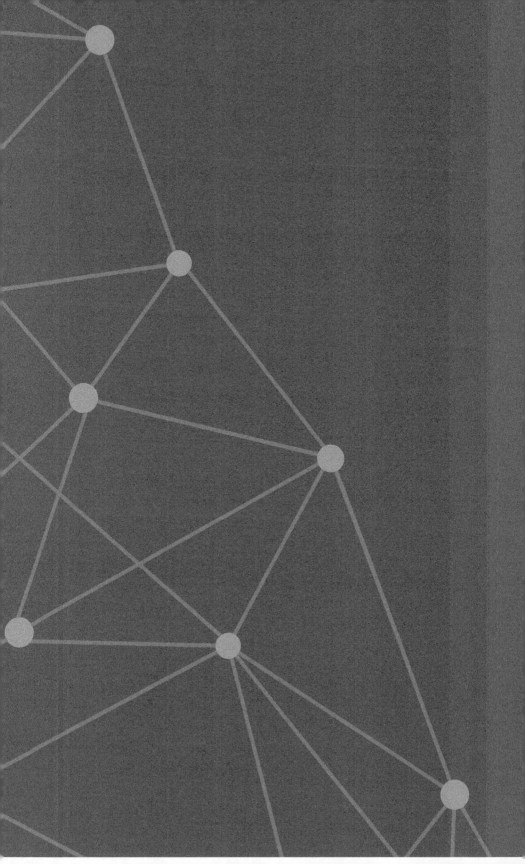

CHAPTER 10

STAGE 5—PREVENT

Preventing is a combination of the right team members taking proactive actions to keep an incident, tragedy, or other costly consequence from happening. The preventing stage is also focused on utilizing lessons learned from other incidents and tragedies and making changes so an organization or community does not make the same mistakes in the future and can more effectively identify and eliminate their gaps, silos, and disconnects.

To effectively prevent violent incidents and tragedies from happening, a paradigm shift in thinking and prevention strategies is needed. This shift requires understanding that first responders are not trained to be first preventers and that responding faster is not the same as proactive prevention.

Responding faster is important and can certainly save lives and damage, but lessons learned from hundreds of attacks show that loss of life and massive damage can take place in a very short period of time. For example, at the Route 91 Harvest music festival on the Las Vegas Strip in Nevada, a shooter killed 58 people and wounded 422 in only minutes before committing suicide. The shooter in Dayton, Ohio, was confronted by law enforcement in less than thirty seconds, but still the shooter killed 9 and injured 17 others. A school shooting at Saugus High School in California lasted only sixteen seconds, but the shooter shot 5 classmates, killing 2, before shooting himself in the head.

Everyone will generally agree that

- preventing the next mass shooting is better than responding to it,
- preventing the next suicide is better than responding to it,
- preventing the next child-abuse tragedy is better than responding to it, and
- preventing the next sexual harassment attack is better than responding to it.

For these events and others to change from response situations to preventable situations, it is important to remember that first responders are typically playing defense. They are trained to respond to 911 calls and numerous other incidents and tragedies. They are brave and courageous, and their job is to rush in and try to end the violence or incident that has taken place or is in the process of taking place.

Preventing is far better than responding because preventing is less expensive, less damaging, less chaotic, and less intrusive, and it results in fewer liabilities and long-term consequences. Yet most organizations and communities do not have a First Preventers Program and continue to invest primarily in response, security, and first responders.

First preventers are trained and equipped to play offense and trained to take action long before the violence or tragic event happens.

LEARN FROM THE PAST

Post-incident reports can provide valuable lessons whether they are from your organization or your community or elsewhere. The prevention stage includes collecting lessons learned and applying them to your organization or community.

What lessons could be learned from the Pulse nightclub shooting in Orlando? The FBI had been monitoring the at-risk individual for ten months, but the FBI did not know what the community knew and determined he was not a threat and stopped monitoring him. He then was able to escalate and plan and execute his attack, which killed forty-nine people and wounded many others. What if the FBI had connected with a community-wide TAT as part of a First Preventers Program? What if they could have learned what others in the community knew? Does your community have a central, trusted, and non–law enforcement way for anyone to share what they observe and know about at-risk individuals?

In 2014, a shooter at the University of California, Santa Barbara, killed six people. After the attack, when his manifesto was found posted online, it became clear that the attack had been a long time in planning, and according to the shooter, it could have been prevented. He had been posting troubling videos on YouTube, and his parents saw them and notified law enforcement that he might be suicidal. When the police came to his house, according to his manifesto, he was terrified they would search his room and find his guns and his written plans. They asked him if he had suicidal thoughts, but he was able to convince the police that he was fine, and they left. Afterward, the shooter took down his YouTube videos and resolved to be more careful. "All it takes is for one person to call the police and tell them that they think I'm going to perpetuate a shooting," he wrote. "I would have been thrown in jail, denied of the chance to exact revenge on my enemies." Unfortunately, the police never came back, and the shooter continued to escalate and then executed his plan of attack.

Is your community, university, school, or organization learning and improving your prevention efforts using manifestos? Numerous other manifestos left behind by at-risk individuals reveal gaps and disconnects that allowed them to execute their plans of violence and/or self-harm. Lessons learned can provide your TAT with valuable information that can help you to update policies, procedures, processes, and other efforts within the Six Stages of Proactive Prevention; however, lessons learned are only valuable if they become lessons implemented.

REVIEW CLOSED CASES

If an at-risk individual has been identified but the case has been closed or the at-risk individual is no longer connected with your organization or community, ongoing questions need to be asked and assessed as part of an ongoing prevention effort. For example, Where are they located? Where are they working? Do public records reveal anything? What are they posting on social media? Do family and friends have any new updates or concerns?

Although questions like those just mentioned are asked during the intervention and monitoring stage, ongoing prevention efforts should continue by one or more team members even though the TAT may have determined the at-risk individual has de-escalated or the case has been closed.

In another example of lessons learned, two men were killed in a murder-suicide at an engineering building at the University of California Los Angeles (UCLA) in 2016. The killer was a former student, and the victim was his former thesis adviser. The shooter reportedly had some mental health issues that had impacted his work at UCLA prior to him graduating in 2003. For months prior to the attack, which happened thirteen years later, the shooter had been making hostile comments about his former professor on social media, at one point calling him a "very sick person" and accusing him of stealing his computer code and giving it to another student. The shooter killed his estranged wife in Minnesota where he was living and then drove to Los Angeles to kill his former adviser.

While it can be difficult to follow up with ex-students, ex-employees, and ex-spouses of employees, research has revealed that attackers with previous connections to a school or organization can fall through the gaps if someone is not checking their social media accounts or checking in with their family, friends, or colleagues to learn if the at-risk individual is displaying or redisplaying red flags, warning signs, or other indicators that they are escalating toward aggression, hostility, or violence.

Therefore, to successfully prevent more incidents and tragedies, the preventing stage should define, engage, and assign TAT members or other internal and external resources to perform reviews of previous and closed cases to determine if a known at-risk individual is re-escalating years later.

CONDUCT PREVENTION REVIEWS

The preventing stage is a good time to review previous stages and previous results so updated strategies can be shared with all appropriate TAT members, internal and external, in order to learn from past efforts and improve future prevention results.

For example, a review could help TAT members learn which interview and/or investigation strategies were more successful in gathering new information, which behavioral assessment resources were more successful, which internal resources are available, which community resources are accessible, which expert resources were suc-cessful, which assessment models delivered valuable and empirically proven details involving at-risk individuals, and so on.

> Reviewing prevention successes and failures can be an excellent sources of valuable information.

Case reviews can also identify successes with valuable community resources such as law enforcement, county agencies, mental health facilities, healthcare organizations, nonprofits, and houses of worship. These community resources may require a new and/or updated MOU to make sure approved external resources are in place for future cases.

Reviews may identify new policies and procedures that need to be created or updated and are then included in the ongoing awareness stage, which will be examined in chapter 11.

Reviewing prevention successes and failures can be an excellent source of valuable information. Since preventing 100 percent of incidents and tragedies is not possible, the preventing stage must also include reviews of failed prevention efforts. This means identify-ing which gaps, silos, disconnects, lack of awareness, documentation failures, policy failures, communication failures, information-sharing failures, lack of resources, accountability failures, authority failures, and other challenges and shortcomings led to the failed prevention.

In some cases, prevention reviews and red-flag path reviews should be conducted by external experts to eliminate bias, cover-ups, silos, and conventional "we have always done it this way" thinking. These and other reviews are vital to improving future prevention successes.

Reviews of successes and failures conducted by external experts should be shared with executive leadership and board members for multiple reasons.

First, in order to ensure a clear line of authority, prevention efforts like the First Preventers Program should be the responsibility of executive-level leadership or board members and not the responsibility of a siloed department leader, such as HR or security. Department leaders typically will not have authority over other department leaders. In addition, tension, excuses, blame, turf wars, and other challenges could erupt when reviewing a failed prevention effort. For example, if HR was in charge, they could end up telling security they failed to do their job. If security was in charge, they could end up accusing HR of failing to do their job. A failure to cooperate becomes a failure to prevent, which gives rise to more gaps, silos, and disconnects. Therefore, every First Preventers Program needs to be the responsibility of executive-level leadership and not a siloed department.

Second, the reviews of successes should be shared with the executive-level leadership team so they can better understand what processes are working or not working and have the authority to adjust the budget to add appropriate prevention resources and make sure proactive prevention continues to be possible.

Third, reviews of failures are vital to making improvements and avoiding the same mistakes in the future. Learning from failures is a lesson learned; not learning from failures is a lesson wasted.

LEVERAGE DATA ANALYTICS

Advanced data analytics is a powerful and proven way to improve proactive intervention and prevention results. Advanced data analytics can help identify trends, patterns, and anomalies that are extremely valuable to adjusting proactive intervention, disruption, and prevention strategies, as well as strategies, policies, and procedures for current and future prevention efforts.

Advanced data analytics can help first preventers be more effective in many ways, and this goes much deeper than just adding up how many incidents occurred, which is what most compliance and audit reporting requirements consist of.

For example, if an organization had one hundred incident reports on workplace violence in the first six months of the year and had ninety incident reports in the last six months, is it safe to assume that workplace violence is down by 10 percent? What else could it mean? What if the second six-month period did not include reports from HR or from a hotline service or from another incident-reporting silo? Any of these could be reason for the reduction in incident reports. What if employees quit filing incident reports because they saw no actions were taken when they reported workplace violence incidents previously? What if the analytics revealed a majority of workplace violence incidents were verbal attacks in the first six-month period, and most of the incidents in the second six-month period were physical attacks? Even though the total number of incidents recorded was lower, could incidents, situations, and individuals be escalating?

Just looking at the total number of incidents can be misleading, which is why advanced data analytics is essential and why data from collecting, assessing, connecting, intervening, and monitoring must be centrally maintained for organizations and communities to perform advanced data analytics and improve their prevention results.

FIRST PREVENTERS AND PREVENTING

Preventing more incidents and tragedies is possible when TAT members from organizations and communities are following up on closed cases, proactively learning, implementing lessons learned, adapting their strategies, using innovative technology, conducting advanced data analytics, and making sure they have TAT members focused on these and other efforts during the preventing stage.

To maintain a successful First Preventers Program, the information from the preventing stage must be coordinated and shared as ongoing awareness with people at all levels across organizations and communities. The ongoing awareness stage will be examined in the next chapter.

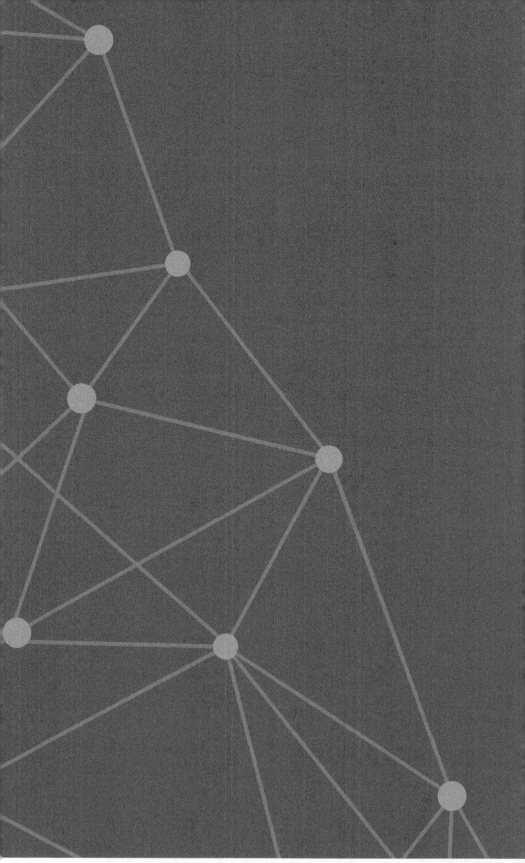

CHAPTER 11

STAGE 6—MAINTAIN ONGOING AWARENESS

The Gilroy Garlic Festival shooting in California on July 28, 2019, resulted in four deaths and thirteen injuries. Five days later, a shooting at an El Paso shopping center in Texas left twenty dead and more than twenty injured. The day after that, a shooting at a bar in Dayton, Ohio, left ten people dead (one was the shooter) and twenty-seven injured.

The frequency of violent incidents, shootings, suicides, and other tragedies in society today is a wake-up call to change the status quo and rethink prevention. The frequency of incidents and tragedies and the increasing number of at-risk individuals who are undeterred by security represent clear indicators that we need to start paying more attention to what evildoers and at-risk individuals are saying and doing (behaviors) and then taking the right actions before they execute their plans.

As mentioned throughout this book, post-incident reports show that evildoers and at-risk individuals, more often than not, give away their plans in advance. As with most other acts of violence, red flags were observed before the attacks in Gilroy, El Paso, and Dayton. In

Ohio, ex-girlfriends and band members said the shooter had begun to talk about dark subjects. Former classmates remembered how the shooter had a hit list, a dismember list, and a rape list in high school and that he was arrested by police on a school bus. Other former classmates said, "We predicted he would do this ten years ago."

Just as it takes a village to raise a child, it takes a community to make and keep a community safe. These red flags and warning signs remind us that ongoing awareness is critical to the effort of intervening and disrupting the attackers and those who are at risk to themselves. Yes, it is a big task, but organization and community safety is possible when executives, employees, TATs, sources, resources, and the whole community have ongoing awareness on their first preventer options and roles so everyone can do their part.

FOCUS ON THE *ONGOING*

There is a very good reason why the final stage of proactive prevention is purposely called "ongoing awareness"—because annual awareness and conventional check-the-box awareness is not enough and not working. Ongoing awareness is critical in order to eliminate common and dangerous awareness gaps that can otherwise lead to embarrassing, costly, and tragic incidents and tragedies.

Ongoing awareness involves all first preventers within organizations and the community at large, who need to be aware and supported by the latest updates of policies, procedures, guidelines, call lists, resources lists, tools, and strategies related to the First Preventers Program. Ongoing awareness should also include ongoing updates on the latest threats, risks, and events that need additional attention.

There are a number of ways ongoing awareness and reminders can be accomplished with in-person training, online training, policy updates, alerts, and other notifications. For organizations and communities, it is important to hold ongoing joint press conferences with law enforcement, community leaders, and even TAT leaders to share awareness and reminders of how to use the butterfly icon so media, nonprofits, and others in the community can all do their part with improving safety and being connected with the First Preventers Program.

People don't know what they don't know, which is why ongoing awareness is needed to eliminate dangerous awareness gaps. Ongoing awareness needs to involve more than just sending information out to employees and others. For example, during awareness updates, press conferences, or assemblies, remind people about First Preventers surveys and other feedback options. Surveys are a great way to identify concerns, challenges, awareness gaps, compliance, fears, threats, and safety issues. Survey data can also be included in advanced data analytics efforts to provide even more visibility for management, TATs, boards, and other key decision makers. Surveys also help people become familiar with the butterfly icon and how easy it is to access it and become a first preventer.

STAY AWARE OF VIRAL THREATS AND TRENDS

Maintaining awareness of viral risks and threats can be a challenge, but awareness of potential risks in the community is important. Take smoking alcohol, for example. Do you know about this potential risk? Kids take an empty two-liter plastic soda bottle and pour in a couple inches of alcohol. They cork the top, stick an air pump needle through the cork, and pump air to pressurize the bottle. They then pop the cork and suck vaporized alcohol through their mouths to get drunk faster. Unfortunately, kids have ended up in comas or dead as a result. Parents or teachers may overhear kids say they are going to "smoke alcohol" and not understand the potential risk if they are unaware.

Another example is the garbage bag challenge. Kids get inside a garbage bag and suck the air out with a vacuum cleaner, which creates a vacuum and the look of a skintight bodysuit, without realizing it can lead to suffocation and brain damage if they try this with their head inside the bag. Other risks include synthetic drugs, counterfeit pills made with fentanyl, vaping, and other real and even deadly risks.

Ongoing awareness efforts should include reminders for your organization as well as the community at large about how to recognize viral threats and how to make incident reports (confidential and anonymous) by simply clicking on the butterfly effect icon. Ongoing awareness should include updates for TATs on how to assess, investigate, intervene, and prevent new and viral risks.

Significant events and threats like the COVID-19 global pandemic will also require new and updated policies, procedures, and strategies for organizations, TATs, community-wide TATs, and communities to include in their ongoing awareness efforts. While a crisis like COVID-19 can be painful and challenging, lessons learned and especially lessons implemented can be extremely valuable for the next crisis.

CULTIVATE COMMUNITY AWARENESS

Anyone in the community can be a hero. Anyone in the community can be a first preventer, but only if community members are aware of what to do when they observe a red flag and only if TATs are aware of what they must do once a red flag has been reported.

For example, it was reported that the mother of the El Paso shooter called the police a week before the attack with concerns that her son had an AK rifle. It was not a crime for her son to have a rifle, so police were limited in any actions they could take. What if police had a way to report all noncriminal red flags to a First Preventers Program? What if noncriminal red flags were automatically shared with community-wide TAT members who could take proactive actions to investigate further, learn more about a parent's concern, and even connect with the potential at-risk individual? What if this lesson learned became a new community policy in their First Preventers Program? Better yet, why is this lesson learned not an ongoing awareness action item and a lesson implemented in communities across the nation?

What if awareness of this lesson learned was shared with your community so the entire community was made aware that simply clicking on a butterfly icon on the website of a school, a house of worship, a nonprofit organization, a hospital, or some other community website would securely and automatically collect their information and share it with first preventers who could take action?

Community members do not have to know to whom precisely they should make an incident report; they only need be aware that the butterfly icon is part of a First Preventers Program that will help make their community safer.

The First Preventers Program is a new and different way for community leaders to help achieve better results when it comes to intervening, disrupting, and preventing violent incidents and tragedies in their community. This is especially helpful with those at-risk individuals who do not have a police record but may pose a risk to themselves and/or others and when community members are the only ones who may be aware of concerning behaviors and suspicious activities.

MONITOR THE CHANGING LANDSCAPE

Attackers are continuously changing and adapting their attack approaches. The Vegas, Gilroy, Dayton, El Paso, and Odessa shootings reveal a scary trend in public places becoming targets of violence. Attackers know there is less security in public places. In Vegas, the attacker was shooting from an elevated hotel room. In Gilroy, the attacker only had to cut through a fence to get into the festival. In El Paso, the attacker just walked right into the shopping center. In Dayton, the attacker walked down the street. In Odessa, the shooter drove around in a car to become a mobile mass shooter.

Organization / School / Higher Education / Etc.	Warning Signs & Red Flags	First Responders	First Preventers Program
Route 91 Music Festival Massacre (Las Vegas, NV)	Yes	Yes	NO
Gilroy Garlic Festival Shooting (Gilroy, CA)	Yes	Yes	NO
First Baptist Church Massacre (Sutherland Springs, TX)	Yes	Yes	NO
Midland-Odessa Mobile Shooting (Odessa, TX)	Yes	Yes	NO
Oregon Historic District Shooting (Dayton, OH)	Yes	Yes	NO
Nova Scotia Mobile Mass Shootings and Fires	Yes	Yes	NO

Based on research from previous attacks, evildoers are studying previous attacks and attacker manifestos and then adjusting their methods for terrorist attacks, workplace violence attacks, dealing drugs, luring youth into trafficking, or cyber and ransomware attacks. Therefore, when new threats and attack methods are discovered, it is vital that the appropriate TAT members are not only made aware of the new risk and attack approaches, but also made aware of updated guidelines and updated actions to take within each of the Six Stages of Proactive Prevention.

As mentioned previously, an increasing number of at-risk individuals who are undeterred by the presence of law enforcement, armed guards, and security measures is changing the landscape for organizations and communities. New strategies and tools like those in the First Preventers Program were developed to more effectively identify, address, and disrupt those undeterred individuals to prevent them from escalating and executing their plans. Has your organization and community updated strategies for the undeterred where conventional intervention and prevention efforts may not be enough?

MONITORING THE LAW

Ongoing awareness should include updates on new and existing state laws, federal laws, and privacy regulations. Organizational and community leaders should utilize their internal and/or external legal expertise to keep TATs updated on an ongoing basis. Ongoing awareness should include compliance, rules and regulations, duty of care, and other safety requirements to ensure TATs are not misguided about what their roles and responsibilities are for different situations.

MONITORING ANALYTICS

Another important ongoing awareness effort comes from reviewing which intervention and monitoring efforts were effective and which were ineffective.[35] This is where the power of data analytics can deliver big benefits.

---

35   Webinars and seminars, such as those offered by SHRM for human resources issues or Dev Resources for K–12 education, are frequently made available online and in person to help teams that want to update

Data analytics applied to intervention and monitoring efforts, such as which actions worked and which didn't work, is one of the best ways to ensure future intervention efforts will be more effective and achieve better results. However, data analytics of which actions worked and didn't work requires the actions and results to be documented and centrally collected so they can be analyzed. Are all your intervention and monitoring actions available for data analytics?

Unfortunately, data analytics is one of the most underutilized efforts in ongoing awareness and in helping TATs to connect the dots and prevent more incidents. To take advantage of data analytics, organizations and communities will need to make a joint effort to change from siloed platform/system approaches to a centralized organization-wide and community-wide program to reap the benefits.

MONITORING POLICY AND PLANS

Ongoing awareness should include updates on outdated policies such as zero-tolerance policies, which were a trend several years ago, but they have proven to be too rigid and have created a lot of unintended consequences and liabilities. Does your organization or community still have zero-tolerance policies in your employee handbook?

> A successful First Preventers Program requires a living playbook of policies, procedures, plans, and guidelines.

Ongoing awareness should include response plans, too, such as crisis response plans, emergency response plans, first responder plans, and recovery plans. Preventing 100 percent

and review their intervention and monitoring efforts and learn better procedures.

of incidents is not possible, which means first preventers and first responders must work together when a prevention effort fails. Does your organization or community have updated plans to include first preventers?

A successful First Preventers Program requires a living playbook of policies, procedures, plans, and guidelines. Remember, just having a living playbook is not enough; all appropriate individuals need anytime access to ongoing updates, and they need to be able to acknowledge their awareness too.

THE SOUTHEAST COMMUNITY COLLEGE CASE

Southeast Community College (SCC) is based in Lincoln, Nebraska, and they knew they wanted to improve ongoing awareness for everyone across multiple campus locations and improve their learning environment and culture of safety too. The security department had been struggling with how to improve its awareness of individuals and situations that needed action or monitoring at the Lincoln campus, as well as multiple remote campuses, some more than one hundred miles away. Their conventional and manual methods of managing information were slow, and they struggled with awareness gaps. As a result, SCC found their security, human resources, student affairs, risk, legal, and other departments were in reaction mode and struggling to get ahead of developing issues.

SCC started its new prevention program by sharing awareness about everyone playing a role in creating "a culture of reporting" across the college's campuses. By using this term, SCC was able to make all staff and students aware that they had an active role in helping one another by sharing concerning behaviors and other warning signs. Almost immediately, the SCC TAT began receiving several new incident reports from all campuses, allowing the SCC TAT to help many individuals who were struggling or at risk.

As SCC continued to develop ongoing awareness and data analytics practices, trends began to emerge. For example, they discovered there were more students than previously known who were at-risk or in danger because of anxiety, depression, and other stressors. By focusing on awareness, they helped everyone become more proactive in looking out for one another, and they were able to use the data analytics to justify bringing on a full-time counselor at the main campus and obtain grant money for dealing with and improving their student depression and suicide-prevention efforts.

FIRST PREVENTERS AND ONGOING AWARENESS

Daily headlines make it seem as though violence, shootings, drugs, abuse, gangs, suicides, and other tragedies are out of control and have become the new normal, but awareness of the First Preventers Program and its impressive successes shows how schools, organizations, and communities can be made safer. It is just a matter of taking heart and taking action, because First Preventers can make a difference.

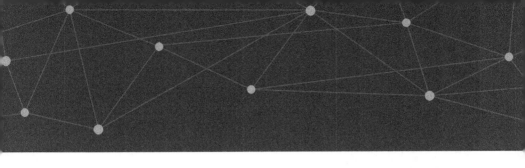

TAKE HEART. TAKE ACTION.

How much longer will we allow children and adults to suffer in fear, pain, and chaos because of incidents and tragedies caused by the increasing numbers of at-risk individuals?

Preventing heartbreaking incidents and tragedies before they occur is possible, but it requires understanding and taking the proactive actions outlined in the First Preventers Playbook.

Everyone has the power to be a first preventer, and anyone can be equipped, trained, and ready to do their part within a First Preventers Program. We simply cannot allow increasing numbers of mass shootings, school violence, workplace violence, community violence, human trafficking, sexual abuse, suicides, and numerous other incidents, attacks, and tragedies to become the new normal.

> Everyone has the power to be a first preventer.

THE NEW NORMAL?

What will this new normal look like? At the time of this writing, we are all experiencing an unprecedented global pandemic due to

COVID-19. Unfortunately, even more people are experiencing fears of the unknown, depression due to stressors, confusion because of misinformation, and chaos because of mass changes. How do we implement programs that are able to adjust, keep pace, and keep people safe?

The COVID-19 pandemic has provided a wake-up call and a serious reminder that when there is no clear cure or vaccine for a deadly virus, people must take proactive actions, the right actions, to do their part in helping to prevent the spread of the virus. As with COVID-19, there is no cure or vaccine for violence, sex abuse, suicides, and numerous other threats, so people must take proactive actions as first preventers to prevent incidents and tragedies from occurring.

THE FIRST PREVENTERS NONPROFIT

Even though most of us want and need better prevention results, common barriers must be eliminated to enable prevention and to protect our most vulnerable loved ones.

For example, it is no secret that schools are struggling with budget cuts and therefore find it difficult to implement more effective and badly needed prevention programs in their schools. The First Preventers nonprofit organization offers creative ways for any school anywhere to implement the research-based and real-world-proven First Preventers Program. Schools can utilize funding sources such as foundations, businesses, sports teams, government grants, public safety grants, associations and parents and crowdfunding options to utilize tax-deductible donations and funds to implement the First Preventers Program.

At FirstPreventers.org, the First Preventers nonprofit helps to guide schools, communities, and organizations through the process of how to take action to improve prevention results.

Ultimately, the goal of FirstPreventers.org is to improve prevention results by delivering research, surveys, assessments, training, experts, technologies, and other preventive intelligence for creating a customized community-wide proactive approach to prevent more incidents and tragedies.

YOU CAN BE A HERO

This book began over twenty years ago when I started questioning why organizations and government agencies were not preventing preventable incidents and questioning what the experts were saying. This book, then, brings you the discoveries of nearly twenty years of research plus over eight years of proven successes that clearly show how the First Preventers Program is preventing more incidents and tragedies.

If you are open minded and would like to be the hero to save lives in your school, organization, government agency, or community, act now. If you would like to be the one who can help deliver peace of mind, more control over safety in the new normal, and a proven program that can deliver one of the highest returns possible—return on prevention—act now. If you would like to be the hero who helps save time, save money, and save your first responders from being in a constant and dangerous response mode, act now.

We cannot afford to sit back and wait for someone else to prevent violence, abuse, suicides, and other incidents and tragedies. Laws, politicians, and security solutions are not delivering the results we need—only the proactive actions taken by first preventers can prevent more incidents and tragedies, as well as prevent the increasing numbers of undeterred at-risk individuals from executing their acts of violence.

Knowing is good, but not enough ... we need to act. Are you ready to be a first preventer?

ABOUT THE AUTHOR

Rick Shaw is a prevention specialist, pathway to prevention thought leader, author, and trusted adviser to organizations and communities. Rick founded Awareity in 2004 and FirstPreventers.org in 2019.

For over twenty years, Rick has been researching post-incident reports, lawsuits, and lessons learned to identify the profile of failed prevention efforts in thousands of targeted violence incidents; workplace, school, and community violence incidents; shootings; suicides; sex abuse incidents; and numerous other tragedies where pre-incident indicators were exhibited and observed. Rick's research exposed a common profile consisting of dangerous gaps, silos, and disconnects that conventional status quo practices and strategies have created.

Using this extensive research, Rick also identified and created the Six Stages of Preventing as well as the first of their kind First Preventers Program and Prevention Platform. The First Preventers Program and Prevention Platform deliver critically needed tools to collect and connect all the right dots and eliminate the dangerous gaps, silos, and disconnects, allowing and empowering communities and organizations to prevent more incidents, tragedies, and other costly consequences, saving lives, reputations, and bottom lines.

Rick's research and leadership has led to thousands of prevention successes, helping to make organizations and communities safer for everyone, especially now.

Printed in the USA
CPSIA information can be obtained
at www.ICGtesting.com
JSHW012033140824
68134JS00033B/3025

9 781642 251258